KIDS

In The

TV COMMERCIAL

BIZ

KIDS

In The

TV COMMERCIAL

BIZ

by

Vernée Watson-Johnson

Illustrated by

Joy Authurine Petrie

Wizards
Production Group

Library of Congress catalog card number 95-62091
ISBN 0-9639824-3-5

Illustrations by: Joy Authurine Petrie
Typesetting: Christine Martin
Cover design: Hollywood Printworks
Publisher: Wizards Production Group–P.O. Box 923252, Sylmar,
        California 91392-3252

*This book is dedicated
to my dear, sweet,
little Mom.*

TABLE OF CONTENTS

INTRODUCTION

This handbook is a step by step guide for children with a desire to do *television commercials* and their parents who are willing to support this desire, realize the financial potential, and who are interested in properly preparing their child for such a career.

Many of you parents have no idea where to begin. You just know you have this **gifted, talented and "personality +"** child whom you believe and have been told **'should be on TV.'** Or your child just has the interest and you're willing to back it.

This handbook gives you and your child the basic information, preparation formula and guidelines to:
– auditioning techniques
– performing ability
– developing a **lasting** career in TV commercials.

It is also a good educational supplement to any theatre or television course and a helpful tool for any child to developing:
– confidence
– self-esteem
– imagination.

Most of the instruction is written directly to the children which aides in the teaching process and a few portions mainly for the parent or teacher. In either case, parental guidance is always a good idea!

Chapter 1

How To

Prepare

• SHOULD THEY OR SHOULDN'T THEY?

Children should do commercial work only if they really want to do it, and their normal development doesn't suffer because of it. For children who are too young to choose, it's up to the parents to set the limitations and decide what is best for their child. Make sure your child is happy and comfortable, and that you do not impose your own desires on them, or push them into a stressful situation.

Older children must be on top of their school work before they can even get a work permit. Be sure that acting is not an excuse for neglecting other responsibilities.

A child has all of their life to work, and should not be concerned about making money or worried as to whether or not they've gotten a job. So don't pressure them about getting the job, or even make that the most important thing. A good audition is an accomplishment within itself and the child first needs to develop strong audition skills without stress. When they do get a job, then you should surely celebrate, but to promise them a surprise or present if they get a job only puts more stress on them for the audition, and even if they did a good audition they will not feel a sense of accomplishment.

There are a lot of factors that go into casting a commercial, so one could have done a wonderful performance at the audition and may not have been chosen because of some other reason: wrong type, not a good match-up with someone else, etc. When they are chosen it's great, although they still have to *do the job*, which is an experience within itself.

There is a lot to consider when deciding to put your child into this business. As with anything, that has potentially great rewards, it takes

– endurance
– commitment
– patience
– and knowledge

on the part of both the **parent** and **child.**

• THE COMMERCIAL TYPE

As far as the **type of children who do well** in the industry, here are a few characteristics that fit the mold. Of course, there are always exceptions to the rule.

− Children who are small for their age.

The industry prefers to use children who are more mature and better able to handle copy and take direction, but who look younger on camera.

− Twins, triplets, etc.

They are often cast because a director can substitute one for the other since legally the amount of time a child can work on the set is limited.

− A child who is independent and secure enough to be away from their parents and work with strangers.

− A child who is outgoing and personable, who ALMOST doesn't know when to "shut up."

− A child who can listen, understand, and do as directed. This is why we emphasize "ALMOST", because even if a child has a great personality and is talkative and expressive, if they can't be quiet or still long enough to take direction and do their performance, then they'll be difficult to work with.

− A child with exceptional reading ability.

As we said before, once in grade school, a child's grades must be up to par before getting a work permit. Since the audition process and the work itself requires lots of reading, fast comprehension and interpretation, it's only to the child's advantage to have strong reading skills.

− A child who is healthy

Children in any area of the entertainment industry need to stay healthy, strong and ready to work. You never know when you'll get a call for an audition. Then once the child starts working the hours are long and require a lot of energy.

Keep them healthy. If you don't have enough knowledge about good nutrition, read some books on the subject. Try to keep your children away from sweets and give them more vegetables and fruit. Watch the processed foods, and read labels to check ingredients. Remember as a parent, you're in charge, so it's up to you what your children eat.

TOOLS

- **TOOLS OF THE TRADE**

Every professional has their tools of the trade. As a performer, your main tools are your **body** and **voice**. These are your PERSONAL TOOLS. You also have your PROFESSIONAL TOOLS like pictures, agents, answering service, etc. We'll get to those in a moment.

First let's focus on your main tools, your body and voice. I've already mentioned *good nutrition*, but you also need exercise in order to maintain a high energy level. Any physical activities like sports, dance classes, martial arts, all help in keeping you in shape and are good ways to develop special skills that you might use in performing.

Right now let's learn some warm-up exercises that you can use to loosen up and get the blood flowing properly and they're a great way of relieving tension right before an audition.

First just take a nice deep breath in through the nose, hold, then let it out through the mouth. Repeat.

- **FACE**

1. An expressive face is a big plus in commercial acting, so let's loosen up and wake up the face.

Start by tightening all the muscles in your face. Shut your eyes tight, squeeze your lips together and pinch your face together as tight as you can. Hold for ten counts.

Now, shake it out — loosely shaking the head from side to side letting all the facial muscles go very loose, blowing out through the lips.

Then repeat the exercise.

This may not look pretty, but it sure wakes up the face and gives you a healthy glow. It also helps keep your face toned for that youthful look.

2. In a chewing, churning motion, rotate the cheeks and lips to the front several times then rotate to the back several times keeping tension in the lips and cheeks.

Now rotate cheeks and lips to the right then left and release, blowing through the lips.

- **EYES**

Holding the head still, circle the eyes around, going to the right, then all the way around, then to the left and all the way around.

Then do 4 corners, focusing on the most extreme 4 points that you can see, making a square. Hit those 4 points to the right several times then to the left.

- **NECK AND SHOULDERS**

Keeping the shoulders pulled down, rotate the head slowly to the right several times, really stretching out the neck. Then change direction.

Now hold the head still and rotate just the shoulders to the front a few times then to the back. Then squeeze the shoulders up and hold, then press them down. Now shake them out.

• ALL AROUND BODY STRETCH

1. Spread your feet about three feet apart, turn them out, keep your body facing front. Stretch the left arm over toward the right, reaching for the wall, bounce gently for 8 counts. Stretch to the left side, right arm over, reach and bounce for eight counts.
2. To the back — First turn the feet parallel (straight forward) and release the head to the back, leaning back as far as possible while bouncing gently for eight counts. Keep your hands out front for balance.
3. Now bend over forward, both hands touching the floor if possible. Bounce gently eight counts, knees as straight as possible. Roll up slowly for eight counts and repeat the exercise.

• JUMPING JACKS

These are a great way to wake up or get the energy level up. Starting with feet together, hands down then jumping as high as possible, feet opening up and arms coming over your head, then jump again, feet coming together arms down and together. Do as many as you can.

• SQUEEZE AND STRETCH AND SHAKE

Now squeeze, and tighten every muscle in your body. Squeeze your face, shoulders (pulling down), make fists, squeeze derriere, legs and knees tight, tight, crunch up your toes, hold several counts. Then release and stretch it all out. On your toes, arms up and reaching out to the furthest point, mouth stretched open, eyes wide, tongue out as far as possible — hold several counts then shake it all out. Shake the head loosely, face muscle slack, arms and legs so loose you could "throw them away". Shake it out, very freely, blowing through the lips.

SQUEEZE   STRETCH

You should be feeling pretty good by now. So let's move on to our Voices.

VOICE

Kids, you can be all dressed up, looking cute, face bright, and alive but if your voice is weak and inaudible, it's all for naught. As a performer you should speak up and speak clearly. Commercial auditioning can be very nerve racking and often in tense situations the voice gets very weak.

In order for you to gain voice control so that they can
– project (speak up)
– overcome the nervous voice
– handle copy with lots of dialogue without running out of air
you must learn how to speak from your DIAPHRAGM.

Okay, so what is the Diaphragm?

The diaphragm is the center of your energy and the power behind your voice.

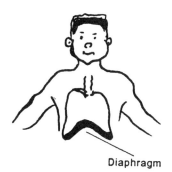

Diaphragm

A horizontal muscle that divides the abdomen and the chest. It goes down to let air into the lungs and up to push air out of the lungs.

Think of the lungs as two balloons. As you put air in, they expand and as you let air out, they deflate. As you pull air in, expand the diaphragm filling up way down in the stomach first, then expand the back, then fill up the chest last, keeping the shoulders down. As you release, you pull in slowly and steadily with your stomach muscles which push the diaphragm up, pushing the air up and out of the lungs at an even flow. YOU DO NOT COLLAPSE THE CHEST. The chest stays lifted while the diaphragm and stomach muscles work.

As you let the air escape out on an even flow, bring it up through the roof of the mouth but in a straight line, pulling the stomach all the way in, slowly. <u>Feel your energy aiming up and out from your center</u>.

Now to strengthen your center of energy, here are some ...

EXERCISES TO STRENGTHEN THE DIAPHRAGM

Throughout the following keep a loose jaw with your throat as loose and open as possible. Speaking from a tight, tense throat is very dangerous and is a misuse of the larynx and vocal cords.

These will require a little knowledge of music, so if you could get access to a piano, pitch pipe or recorder, it would help. However, if you can hit a note in your head and you're able to go up a step, down a step, or run through the octave, then you don't need an instrument.

In commercial acting, because it requires such a range of emotion you'll find yourself using all areas of your voice.

So you should work the full range of your voice in these exercises.

Remember to fill up all the way, chest high, shoulders relaxed.

Let the sound and air come out through the roof of the mouth through a loose relaxed jaw. Keep your hand on your stomach so that as you inhale, you can feel the stomach expand and as you exhale, the stomach pulls in slowly.

HEY

Down and up the scale holding on the high notes and the low note. Make sure you fill up and in one breath on a nice full 'Hey' sound, slide (descending) down to the low note. Hold. Slide (ascending) up to the high note. Hold. The exercise is done *(legato)*, meaning it is done smoothly with one note flowing into the other. If you don't have a piano, start on a note around the same pitch as your normal speaking voice. If you do have one, start on middle C then go down the octave and back up to middle C. Take a breath, fill up, start again on Hey, one step up on D. Down the octave, then back up to D.

These exercises are written in the bass clef because I want you to start in the low tones and ascend throughout the exercise.

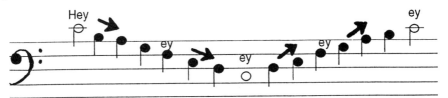

Keep going up one step at a time until your voice reaches its limit. Then start at C again and go down one step at a time to the bottom limit.

If you're working from your diaphragm and keeping a nice loose jaw, the Hey should come out full and rich with a lot of volume behind it. If it sounds weak and shaky, drop the jaw more and try to keep the image of the balloon. As you fill it up, it expands, as the air and sound come out, it deflates (stomach goes in). If you're running out of air, you may either have not taken enough in, let too much out on the 'H' sound, or you're not pulling the stomach in enough toward end.

HUM-M-M

Do the same scales as the exercise before but only this time, to feel your voice placement, close your mouth and hum. Starting on top, holding, slide down the octave, hold, then back up to the top. Hold. If your lips are closed but soft and you're bringing the air up through the roof of your mouth (even though in this case, out the nose), you should feel a tickle in the lips and a vibration in your nose and face. Keep your hand on your stomach to make sure you're working correctly.

B-R-R-R
Using the same scales as the first two exercises, blow the air through loose lips giving you a B-R-R-R sound. Descend the octave on B-R-R-R then back up holding the last note.

Repeat going one step up each time as high as you can go. This one really works not only the diaphragm, but warms up the lips. It tickles the nose too!

HEY HEY, HI HI, HEY OVER THERE, HI OVER THERE
This exercise is a little different, but it is fun. It combines (staccato) and (legato). Staccato means you don't hold the note. You hit it quickly with lots of energy then you get off of it. This is good for the diaphragm because *between* each and every note in staccato you let the air drop in quickly and *on* the note you push out quickly so the stomach is moving in and out rapidly and getting a good workout.

Now I said this one is a combination. So the first notes are staccato (HEY HEY HI HI), and the last notes are legato (HEY OVER THERE, HI OVER THERE).

Here's some imagery: Imagine yourself high on top of a mountain peak calling to someone on the mountain peak across the valley.

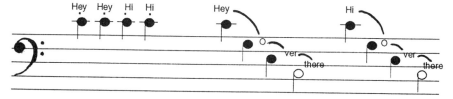

You start with a C major chord, then go to the D major, E major and so on. Putting your hand on your stomach and taking a breath between each, push out. HEY HEY HI HI (hit them – let them go). Now smoothly (legato) descending the chord:
HEY O-VER THERE (Holding THERE)
HI O-VER THERE (Hold as long as possible)

If you don't have a piano, start on a normal speaking tone with

HEY, go down three steps to "O", two steps to "VER", then two steps to "THERE".
"HEY" Being The Top Note of Octave
"THERE" Being The Bottom of Octave

HEY HEE HI HO HOO's (Like A, E, I, O, U)

This is the ultimate diaphragm workout. It may seem complicated but follow along and between the words and music, you'll get the idea. You do one vowel sound at a time with the H in front. They're done quickly, all staccato except the last note.

Going up the scale starting on C (an octave below middle C) skip up a step, go back a step, skip up a step, go back a step, skip up a step, go back a step, skip up a step, go back a step, skip down a step, up a step, skip down a step, down a step, stay and hold. The last note you hold the longest.

Then, still on HEY, start on middle C going basically in one direction this time. C, skip down a step, up a step, skip down a step, up a step, skip down a step, up a step, skip down a step, up a step, skip down a step, up a step, down a step, down a step, stay, Hold. Stop.

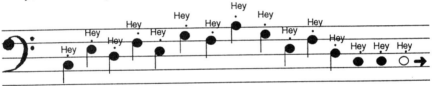

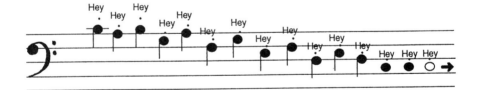

Make sure you're keeping your hand on your stomach to feel it work quickly in and out. Just release out to let the air in and pull in to push the sound out only holding, pulling, all the way in on the very last note.

Now do the same on HEE, then HI, HA, HO, HOO. Then raise the pitch to D, then E, etc. Do as much as you can adding more the next time.

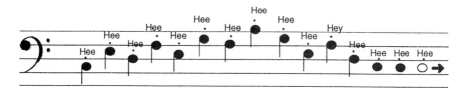

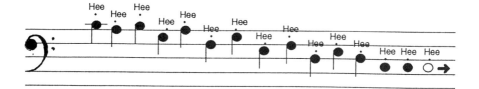

Okay. The voice and diaphragm should be humming by now. If your throat is a little tired just relax it, roll the head and drink some water or hot tea and lemon, but if you're working correctly you should not be hoarse.

THE SPEAKING VOICE

Many of us have a lazy tongue or are just not used to articulating and clearly annunciating every syllable, which is required in most commercial copy. Your dialogue in a commercial may have taken months to be written and approved, so each word is important.

Let's work on our speaking voice.

Still using the diaphragm, fill all the way up speaking slowly but say as much as you can before taking another breath. Really working the lips and tongue, pronouncing every vowel, every consonant, the beginning and end of each word, try these fun tongue twisters:

During these exercises use a tape recorder to record your voice and listen to the playback carefully. Circle your trouble spots with a pencil and work on them. Only erase the circles when you have corrected that spot.

The tip of the tongue
the teeth
the lips

Say it slowly making sure you pronounce **the beginning and end of each word.**

Try these:

Archibold Agarway arched his eyebrows with an axe. OUCH!

Read these slowly, breaking up the unfamiliar words so that you say them correctly with all the syllables.

Danny Dobbs blows double bubbles in the Hubble Street Bubble Band.

Donald Dutchmire dumped his dog in the ditch. DANG!

*Make sure you pronounce the p's and d's.

Francis Funkleroy fought a fantastic feat and finished first in the fierce feather fight.

Jimmy Jamboree jumped and jiggled to the jukebox.

Do these very dramatically and have fun with them. Do them slowly but with lots of energy, using the mountain peak image we used in "Hey Over There". Or do them crisp and quickly like a schoolteacher or a news reporter. Make up some of your own. You can practice your articulation by reading OUT LOUD any book, newspaper, magazine commercial ads, school reports, whatever!

Your body and voice should be in good shape by now so let's move on to

YOUR PROFESSIONAL TOOLS

- **WARDROBE**

On the majority of calls the agent will say they just want "nice casual."

NICE CASUAL – Something neat and comfortable that goes along with the current trends. Set aside a couple of clean, well-fitting, casual outfits that stay in good shape for audition purposes – YOUR AUDITION CLOTHES

Unless specifically asked for, don't wear sloppy or torn clothing, stay with the neat look. Girls be careful not to dress too maturely for your age.

- **PICTURES**

Just starting out all a child needs is a 3 x 5 or 5 x 7 snapshot. It could be a headshot, 3/4 shot, or full length in a nice casual outfit. Parents, if you're taking a full length snapshot of your child, make sure it's close enough that the child's features are clearly seen. The snapshot can be in color or black and white. Have copies made and keep track of the negatives in case you need more.

Now staple the snapshot to a plain piece of paper with the child's *name, date of birth, social security number, current height and weight, eye color, hair color, clothes size, special skills if any, like dancing, singing, sports, etc., and a phone number where you can be reached.* (See example pg. 14)

Name —————————————— **D.O.B.** ————

SS# ———————————— **Ht.** ——— **Wt.** ———

Eye ——— **Hair**—— **Clothes Size** ———

Contact # ————————————————

Special Skills ————————————

You use these to mail to prospective agents, we will discuss in a moment, but let's stick with pictures.

Once you get an agent you may be able to use these snap-shots for a while, but soon you will have to get new pictures. The business is ever changing and so it is with the style of picture they use. Composites were the thing for a long time (see example pages) but recently it has been simplified to a single 8 x 10 headshot or 3/4 shot.

JOSH ELLIOTT JOHNSON

D.O.B. : 8-24-87
S.S.#

YOUNG PEOPLE'S DIVISION

Joseph
Heldfond &
Rix, Inc.

1717 N. Highland Ave., L.A., CA 90028
213/466-9111 • FAX 213/466-3352
A KAZARIAN-SPENCER-PITTS CO.

PAPER CHASE PRINTING INC. 213/874-2300

KELLEN
HEIGHT: 45"
HAIR: BROWN
EYES: GREEN
D.O.B.: 10-23-87

L.A. KIDS
A DIVISION OF LA MODELS
L.A. MODELS • 8335 SUNSET BLVD., LOS ANGELES, CA 90069 • (213) 656-9572 • FAX (213) 656-0489

L.A. TALENT

L.A. TALENT • 8335 SUNSET BLVD LOS ANGELES CA 90069 • (213) 656 3722 • FAX (213) 650 4272

(310) 439-5661

ARIELLE DORSEY
HAIR: BROWN EYES: BROWN
D.O.B.: 9-30-91 SS#:

PAPER CHASE PRINTING INC 213-874-2300

COURTNEY
MUN

11365 Ventura Blvd. Suite 100, Studio City, CA. 91604
818/769-9111 • FAX 818/755-7553
YOUNG PEOPLE'S DIVISION
FORMERLY JOSEPH HELDFOND & RIX

Kazarian
Spencer &
Assoc., Inc.

Your agent will advise you as to the type of photo they use and they should also refer you to a good photographer.

CHOOSING A PHOTOGRAPHER

If you want to get the BEST person for the least amount of money, you have to shop around. As I mentioned, the agent your child signs with is the best source but you can also ask friends or check the TRADE papers for photographer advertisements. When you choose a few, call and set up an appointment for an interview first.

- **THE INTERVIEW**

Look through the photographers book to see:
- the quality of their work
- other children's photos they've done
- do they work well with children

Check out the environment
- Is it comfortable for you and your child
- Will the child feel safe and at ease
- If you wish, ask if they provide music
- Will it be indoor or outdoor shooting so you can prepare properly.

- **PRICE**

For the session and for the prints ... What does the price include?

- **HAIR**

A neat, casual, simple style.   The same way that it will probably look in auditions. Be sure to keep the hair out of the face. If you have bangs, keep them cut. You want the child to look like the picture when they walk in.

- **MAKE-UP**

Very minimal, if any at all. Maybe just a light base or tissue to wipe the shine down, and keep the lips moist (no color).

- **WARDROBE**

Nice casual is best. Always take plenty of choices and between you and the photographer you can decide which works best. You may even decide to try two different looks.

- **THE SESSION**

–Parents make sure your child is well nourished, well rested and well groomed for the shoot day.

–Plan to arrive early.

–Plan or prepare a snack and a lunch if it's going to be a long day.

–Take their favorite music along, keep them in a good mood and have fun.

- **PROOFSHEETS**

A few days after the session the photographer will give you proofsheets or contact sheets. They'll contain all the pictures from the session (see example).

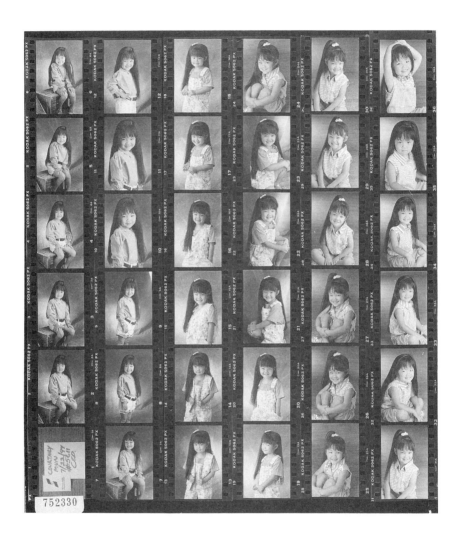

From those you choose which ones to enlarge to 8 x 10 prints. If you already have an agent then they should have the final decision since they know what kind of pictures work and what casting directors are looking for.

Don't go crazy ordering 10 or 15 prints if you had a great session. Narrow it down to a few shots with different looks. If it was a bad session, just print one or two and see what you've got!

• REPRODUCTIONS

Usually the agent will advise you as to where to get copies of the chosen print made and request the agency logo to be printed on them also. Otherwise, get referrals or check the TRADES for places to do 8 x 10 repros.

The Repros should
–have the child's name printed on the front
–have agency logo (if signed)
–be of good quality paper
–closely resemble the print in tone and contrast.

Always keep the agent supplied with pictures so that they can have something to work with and represent your child properly. So keep TRACK OF THE NEGATIVES. Know where they are and how to get a hold of them so you can get more copies done quickly when you need them. Often times the photo reproduction house holds on to the negatives so that all you need to do is call to order more.

• UPDATING

Children change and grow so quickly so you may need to update and get new pictures in a year or two. Realize this possibility so that you can financially plan for the event.

That's it for pictures!!

• RESUMÉS

Most children starting out don't need a resumé. But once you get some experience you should put together a professional looking resumé with the following information: name, contact

number, height, weight, SS#, color of eyes and hair, union affiliation, skills and training if any. Even though it is not a prerequi-
site, you can include your theatre, television and film experience,
if any. If you have done commercials they should <u>NOT</u> be listed.
This avoids any concerns about competitive products. (See note
pg. 57) Just state "Commercials upon request" or "Commercial
tape available".

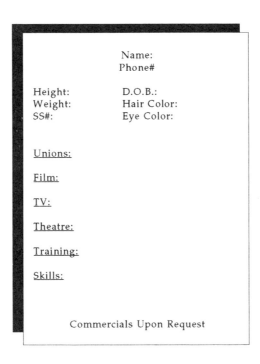

```
                              Name:
                              Phone#

          Height:             D.O.B.:
          Weight:             Hair Color:
          SS#:                Eye Color:


          Unions:

          Film:

          TV:

          Theatre:

          Training:

          Skills:



              Commercials Upon Request
```

• SOCIAL SECURITY NUMBER

Your child cannot work without it. Get your child a social
security card and keep the number with you, or better still,
memorize it.

• WORK PERMIT

State Labor Laws require that all children under 18 years of
age acquire a work permit before working, and you, as a parent,
should be responsible to get it, renew it and keep it current.

According to the requirements of your state or the state office where you apply, you'll need,

the child's birth certificate

possibly a doctors note

and school record

Work permits are only good for a limited amount of time, usually six months. Find out where the State Office Building is, get a copy of your child's birth certificate, and school records if they are school age and apply for the permit. It only takes one or two days to get and the first thing an agent asks is "Does the child have a social security number and work permit?" So get them and keep them handy!

• ANSWERING SERVICE

This is a very important connection. Have a service number, answering machine, paging system or voice mail where you can receive a message and check it often. It's pretty frustrating to miss out because you didn't check your service.

• AN AGENT

An agent/agency acts as your representative in the commercial industry. When you sign with an agency, both parties sign standard union contracts from the Screen Actors Guild (SAG) and AFTRA. Basically, it states that they will represent you commercially (send you on auditions, negotiate your deals, and sell you as a client), in exchange for 10% of your gross income of the jobs you book through them. **They are working for you. You are working for yourself and with them.**

You can only sign with one commercial agent at a time. Some times children don't have to sign but just register with an agent and they will still send you out. The same 10% applies. Be careful of becoming involved with so-called agents, managers or schools that charge you large fees to get your child in the business.

• GETTING AN AGENT

1. Get a list of **union franchised agencies** from a theatrical bookstore that includes information on:

   a. type of agency

b. who works in the different departments

c. what type they represent

Some lists also give information about sending in pictures/ calling/general auditions, etc. Each agency is set up differently. Some of them have departments that cover other areas of the commercial industry in which you may be interested. For example, print, voice, theatrical, dance, directing, and others.

Choose the ones you think will fit your needs, but make sure they are SAG franchised agents.

Then **Do Mailings**

If you have an 8 x 10 shot fine, if not, use the snapshot layout that we talked about in Professional Tools giving all of your child's information.

Also include a note stating that you are looking for representation for your child and, if you have been referred, be sure to give the persons name who referred you.

In a couple of weeks make follow-up calls and say that you've sent in your child's picture and you would like to make an appointment for an interview, or just make contact and see when you should call back.

• INTERVIEW WITH THE AGENT

Parents, you should set up interviews with several agents before you make a choice, unless they come highly recommended.

At the interview you should find out

–how their office is set up, the procedures for their clients

–who works in the different departments

–other children they represent, especially in your child's category.

• THE CHILD'S INTERVIEW WITH THE AGENT

At one point during the interview, the agent may ask to talk to the child away from the parent. In preparing your child for a meeting with an agent or casting director, tell them that the people they'll be talking with are friends, and they may ask them some questions, or have them do a practice commercial. They should just *talk freely, relax, listen, have fun,* and *be themselves.*

Once you get an agent, this is how the process works: The agent receives breakdowns from commercial casting directors (CD's) or producers, describing the type or types they need for a particular spot.

If it's your category, the agent submits your picture along with others in your category and if you're one of the ones chosen by the CD, you get a call from your agent for an audition, to see if you're right for the job.

Generally, you will not be called to audition unless you're submitted by an agent.

WORKING WITH YOUR CHILD

In preparing for the agent interview and the actual audition process here are some ways to work with your child.

• WARM-UP

Before you get started, warm-up with some of the body and voices exercises that we did earlier.

• PRACTICE READING WITH INTERPRETATION

If your child is old enough to read, you can use commercial advertisements or the Practice Commercials in Chapter 2 of this book. Work on articulation as we did in the warm-ups, making sure all the words are pronounced correctly.

Then have him read it again, this time paying **attention to punctuation.** This is an important aspect in getting the basic meaning of what is being read and reading with the right inflections. So let's go over their meaning.

? Question Mark – The voice goes up at the end of a sentence.

. Period – the end of a thought or statement, the voice goes down.

, Comma – Not the end of a thought, but connects to something else and the voice goes up.

. . . Ellipsis– You don't really finish your statement or question. It trails off or is interrupted. Have the child create the rest of the sentence (continue the thought) as if they were not interrupted. But make sure they know the sentence is supposed to be cut off.

!!! Exclamation – Very up, excited, surprised, happy, emphatic, or angry.

You may not come across all of these on the same piece of copy but as you work, take note to pay attention to them.

Also, instead of just reading words, try to interpret the thoughts and emotions behind the words.

This method of doing a **Copy Breakdown** aids in understanding and expressing what you're reading.

1. Decide what the overall thought is behind the spot, what method of selling are they using, "hard sell" or "soft sell."

2. What do they want you to think or feel about the product?

3. What are the descriptive words or phrases?

4. Are there any changes in thought or emotion – **Transitions.**

5. Is the product compared to another product? Are there any objections being made?

6. What are the benefits of the product?

All of these questions may not apply all the time but they give you a good basis for breaking down copy.

Think of your reading as a little performance. Once you have figured out the copy then it's time to add some ELEMENTS to your performance.

PERFORMANCE ELEMENTS

The following elements add levels, colors and expression to your performance.

• FOCUSING

This means to clear your mind of any distractions or unrelated thoughts and just think about what you are saying and doing in the spot. Commercial acting is very technical and your specific dialogue and action are very important. This leaves no room for thinking about other things like what you look like, what you're going to do afterwards, etc..
Remember to stay Focused.

• ARTICULATION

Pronounce the words clearly and correctly unless you are directed to do otherwise. Work on the words or phrases that give you trouble, until they flow easily. Except for practice, you don't have to over pronounce the words like we did in the exercises, but use correct pronunciation in a natural way as if this is the way you speak all the time. Keep your lips and tongue relaxed and flexible so they can work properly and use the **diaphragm.** If you have a lot of copy, be aware not to gasp for air between phrases but lift up and let the air drop in, filling up quickly through a loose mouth without making noise.

• CREATIVE EXPRESSION

Have fun with it! Using your creativity you should express yourself giving different levels and colors to your performance. It is important in commercial acting for you to be very expressive, almost bigger than life in some cases. It helps to imagine that you're painting a picture with your words, giving them more meaning and variety in tone, but remember to keep it believable. We have to believe what you are saying. Again, use your diaphragm so your voice won't crack or go way up in your head. Be expressive and let the creative juices flow.

• **SPONTANEITY**

This means to make your performance sound spontaneous and unrehearsed. This really applies when you have to repeat your performance over and over. Keep it fresh, like you just came up with it at the moment. Just let it happen!

• **TRANSITION**

Going from one thought to another, a change in thought which creates a change in attitude. As you read the copy, connect the thoughts that should be connected but when there's a change in thought, make it clearly and smoothly so that the copy flows and makes sense.

By doing a copy breakdown and using your performance elements, your reading should have more life, flow easier and sound more natural.

We will be using these techniques in Chapter 2 on our practice commercial copy, but for now, Let's move on to memorizing the material.

MEMORIZATION

Often commercial acting requires quick memorization. The more familiar you are with the copy the easier it is to memorize it.

HOW TO MEMORIZE

−Figure out the thoughts behind the lines so you're not just saying lines but thinking the thought and remembering from one thought to another, instead of just one word or one line to another.
−Repeat the lines over and over thinking and connecting the thoughts.
−Trouble Spots - if you have a spot that gives you trouble do this:

Say the line before the trouble spot

Then say the line you're having trouble with

Then the line after the trouble spot

Just work that section until it flows easily.
Practice memorizing different material that you are unfamiliar with. The more you practice the easier and faster you can develop memorization skills.

However, there may be many times when you won't be able to memorize. For instance:
    – At a commercial audition when they take you in right away.
    – There's too much copy for you to memorize quickly.
    – You're handed something at the last minute at an audition or agency interview.

So for the above you need to develop your

COLD READING SKILLS

We've already done some of the cold reading skills. They include:
    – paying attention to punctuation
    – finding the thoughts behind the words
    – connecting thoughts
    – reading with interpretation and meaning

Practicing these techniques are your cold reading basics. But all this does you little good if you're looking down at the paper and no one can see your face. So let's learn

THE DELIVERY TECHNIQUE

Which means that instead of looking at the material you're reading while saying the lines.

You quickly
    – look at the material
    – read a phrase at a time, getting the thought behind it
    – absorb it

Then deliver the line (say the line) to:
    – a camera's eye (if you have a home video)
    – a tape mark on the wall like

this   —or—   this

– or the person you're speaking to.

In other words you read the line quickly to yourself, then look right back into the camera, or to the mark on the wall or the person you're speaking to.

Treat the 'camera' or 'mark on wall' as a 'Person'. Like you're talking to a friend. This will help you to be more natural.

This delivery technique lets others see your expression and get more meaning from what you're saying.

• **CUE CARDS**

In commercial acting quite often the material or copy (which it is called) is written not just on paper but also on CUE CARDS when you get into the audition room. Cue cards are large white cards or large sheets of paper with the commercial copy handwritten on it. They are usually placed across the room from the actor, someplace close to the camera so you can refer to them easily.

To practice reading from cue cards,

1. Get some poster size white cards or a large pad about 2-1/2' long x 2' wide.

2. Clearly write the practice commercial on it. Using a bold, dark colored marker to write with is best.

3. Set the cue card standing up against something, put it close to the 'camera' or 'mark on wall.'

Practice using the delivery technique with the CUE CARD. In doing this, you have to get used to the way the words are placed on the card as opposed to the paper.

In writing the CUE CARD try not to space the commercial exactly the way it's spaced on the paper since in auditions the **copy on paper looks different from the copy on a cue card.**

Let your eyes get used to referring to cue cards and focusing back into the camera. This is another important technique to practice.

Before we move on, let's learn the **Stage Areas** and how they relate to

CAMERA DIRECTIONS

so that you will be able to take directions properly and know which way to move.

In doing plays you need to know the areas of the stage so you'll know how to move "Stage left" or "Stage right", etc.

In commercial acting the same terms are sometimes used, but more often you'll hear 'camera right' or 'camera left' which is the direct opposite from the stage so let's learn both.

• **STAGE AREAS**

This is from the actor's point of view facing the camera or audience.

Let's say you're on stage or in the playing area at an audition, and you're facing the camera or audience. If you're asked to move:

Stage right – you would move to your right

Stage left – you would move to your left

Upstage – move backwards toward the back wall - away from the camera or audience

Downstage – move forward toward the camera or audience

Center stage – you would move to the center or middle of the stage or playing area

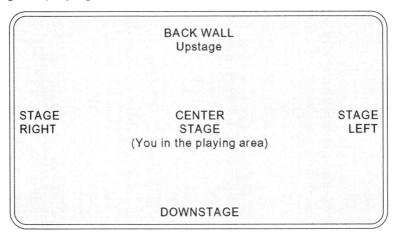

BACK WALL
Upstage

STAGE   CENTER   STAGE
RIGHT   STAGE   LEFT
                (You in the playing area)

DOWNSTAGE

CAMERA / AUDIENCE

In commercial acting - Stage areas are more often referred to as 'YOUR' ... like "move to your left" or "move to your right" which is exactly what it means.

• CAMERA DIRECTIONS

Like I said, camera directions are the direct opposite. Camera Directions are from the camera's point of view looking at the actor.

So if you're in the playing area, you are **facing the camera** and you're asked to move.

Camera Right – you would move to <u>your left</u>

Camera Left – you would move to <u>your right</u>

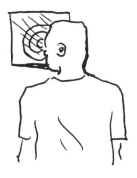 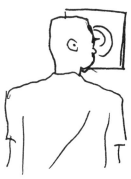

Stage right   **Stage left**
Camera left   **Camera right**

Now they don't say 'up camera' or 'down camera' but

Away from Camera – move further away from the camera

Toward Camera – come closer to the camera

Toward camera   **Away from camera**

Don't make LARGE QUICK movements (unless otherwise directed)

Move a little at a time until the director gets what he or she wants.

Practice moving to these areas.

Parents can call out the area that the child should move to. Call them in different order. Keep going over them until they become second nature.

- **PANTOMIME**

This is another technique you will need to know before auditioning. You've probably done it lots of times but didn't know it was called pantomime.

Pantomime is working with objects that aren't really there. Say you are asked to drink a glass of water at an audition and you didn't actually have a glass in your hand, you have to **act as if** (pretend) **you did** and create the glass from your memory and imagination.

- **PRACTICE ON PANTOMIME**

1. Practice doing simple actions with the actual objects first (see pg. 38). As you do the action **be especially aware** of:
    − the size, weight and texture of the object
    − how it fits in your hand
    − what your body is doing during the action

2. Put the object aside and do the same action using **pantomime.**
    Remembering:
    − the size, weight and texture
    − the way it fit in your hand
    − what your body was doing

Remembering all of these things is called
SENSE MEMORY

Using your sense memory to do Pantomime, recreate the objects and do the actions **"as if"** they were really there.

• **Pantomime GUIDELINES**

So that objects don't appear as if they have disappeared from your hands, or fallen, or gone through something – here is a simple rule to remember while doing pantomime.

Each action in pantomime has a Beginning, Middle and End

The Beginning – is when you pick the object up, lift it or move it

The Middle – is when you're using the object, or putting it on

The End – is when you put the object down, release it, pass it over, eat it or take it off

If your pantomime involves eating something, this has it's own beginning, middle, and end - - separate - - but coming out of getting the food.

The beginning is the bite, or putting it in your mouth.

The middle is tasting and chewing the food

The end is swallowing the food.

The following are just a few examples of Pantomime and Mime actions you may be asked to do, and good practice for understanding the technique.

Practice Pantomimes

1. Drinking something from a glass or bottle or container. All are different.
2. Combing or brushing your hair *
3. Brushing your teeth
4. Reading a book, newspaper or magazine (notice the difference in size and the way you turn the pages)
5. Writing a note
6. Putting on a coat, hat, etc.
7. Pouring and eating cereal
8. Playing a video game
9. Eating a hamburger or hot dog *
10. Working on a computer

* Make sure you're aware of the difference when you're using different objects.

Or you may be asked to do

MIME

Which is another form of pantomime but in mime you are also creating space or conditions that aren't really happening.

Like:
1. Being hot or cold.
2. Riding in a crowded bus
3. Playing basketball
4. Watching television
5. Dancing to no music

The same rule applies in Mime.
Each action has a beginning – middle – and end.

Beginning – start of the action (getting on the bus, stepping out in the cold, etc.)

Middle – Your body's movement or reaction to the activity condition, or force. (like the shivers in the cold, or being crunched on a bus; being blown by the wind, etc.)

End – Coming to the end of the action. (getting off the bus; coming in from the cold, etc.)

Here's an exercise *in moving through space* that can help with changes in the environment.

SPACE EXERCISE

1. Clear an area for yourself where you can walk around freely and not bump into anything. We start with a light environment, changing slowly to a heavy atmosphere back to light. Walk around the room. Imagine the surrounding air being very light with a nice warm breeze blowing, very easy to move through and very comfortable. It begins to get a little misty and cloudy. Now the air is getting thick with no breeze and it's not as easy to move through or to breathe. It begins to get very stuffy, thick, dirty, and hot (like L.A. smog or N.Y. humidity). You are extremely uncomfortable. Finally, it begins to let up a little (very little at first). There is a slight movement in the air, and your breathing is getting easier. It's getting clearer and clearer and a breeze is beginning to blow more and cool you off. Finally, the air has lightened up again and you can move freely and feel much better.

2. Now do the same exercise and instead of the air going from light and warm to thick and hot, it goes from light and warm to thick and cold. It gets so cold and heavy that you can hardly move, and in the freezing air, it hurts to breathe. From this extreme it begins to ease up slowly and get a little warmer as your body loosens up a little until you are completely comfortable and moving freely.

The main thing in this exercise is to go through it very slowly and to really feel the changes in your space.

The best way to develop a sense memory for mime and pantomime is to be more aware of the elements around you, and how your body reacts in certain conditions. As you go through your daily life, take note of your **body language** as you move from one situation to another or as you use and handle different objects throughout the day.

- **GAME**

You can make up your own pantomime and mime exercises and have the person viewing you guess what you are doing.

They can be simple or complicated like, if you're making a sandwich, be specific as to the type of sandwich and let them guess what kind and what you put on it. But for each action, make sure it has a Beginning – Middle – and End. You can recreate just about any activity and who knows, one of them may be just what you need at an audition.

- **CREATIVE DIALOGUE**

Some auditions have no written copy at all and you may have to make up your own. So, apart from being able to create space, you may and should be able to create your own dialogue in a given situation. For practice, make up a situation where you're telling someone a story. Using the past tense and a lot of imagination, just start talking and keep going. For instance: "I was walking along the street one day and I ran into this friend I hadn't seen in a long time. We were so surprised to see each other. We just stood there with our mouths open and then we just started talking and talking. I told him (or her) about ...." It can go on and on.

–OR–

"You won't believe what happened to me yesterday ..." Or anything else you come up with as long as you keep it going.

Now change to present or future tense. For instance:

"Today is such a busy day. I have a test in social studies, a play rehearsal, then I have to ..."

–OR–

"I know exactly what I'm going to do to start working on my project ..."

The dialogue can begin in hundreds of different ways and can lead to hundreds of different places, but being able to create it on the spot takes practice and the more you work at it, guess what, the better you'll get.

Parents, for two or more children, one starts the dialogue then as you point to another child the one talking stops immediately and the other picks up right where they left off.

This is great practice in **'listening to others'** and for commercials using improvisation, which we will talk about in Chapter 2.

CHAPTER WRAP-UP

In this chapter we have covered the basic skills, tools and exercises needed to prepare you as a performer and professional. Now let's move on to the actual audition process.

Diaphragm

Chapter 2

How To
Get Them

THE AUDITION

What exactly is an audition??

An audition is a trial performance, to determine whether or not you are right for the job.

• **THE GAME PLAN**

The more experience you get at auditioning, the better. Even if you don't get every job you go out on or think you did great on, keep in mind there are a lot of factors that go into booking a job that may not have anything to do with your performance.

My advice is to treat each audition as an experience to learn from. Keep sharpening your tools with each one and get as much experience as possible.

• **WHAT WILL I BE ASKED TO DO?**

For infants, an audition may just entail the baby being put on camera with an actor or actress, playing with a toy, or just being cute. But for older kids you may be asked to do

  – something more specific like a directed action or reaction, or

  – an improvisation.

  – one word

  – lots of dialogue

  – interacting with other performers

But before we talk about the performance part of the audition, let's discuss what happens first.

When you get
THE CALL

from your agent for an audition, get as much information as possible (parents take note), as to:

1. WHERE IT IS

- KNOW WHERE YOU'RE GOING:

If the address of the audition is unfamiliar to you, ask your agent what it's near, or better still, get a Thomas Guide and look it up so you'll know exactly where you are going and how to get there. If you have more than one audition, you should plan your route between them, keeping in mind traffic, distance, and parking time, especially if they're scheduled close together. As you go along, make yourself familiar with the parking conditions and regulations in the surrounding areas. This can give you more options and save you money in parking tickets as well as time in finding a spot. And make sure you have coin change for parking meters. Those of us using public transportation, especially in Los Angeles, (New York is not such a problem, just the traffic), check the schedules and make sure you can make the connections.

2. WHAT THE PRODUCT IS:

Get the exact product name and if it is unfamiliar, find out how to pronounce it correctly. Product name is also important because, in the same casting offices, there may be other commercials being cast with other kids, so know <u>what</u> you're going up for.

3. WHAT THEY'RE LOOKING FOR:

Most of the time they may just asked for NICE CASUAL which we've already discussed on page 13, but find out as much as you can about the character type or tone of the commercial like:

lots of excitement
very real
comedic
animated
intellectual
hip

4. IS THERE ANY COPY?

Find out if you will have dialogue in the commercial and if so, plan to arrive early so that you can work on the copy.

AT THE AUDITION

REMEMBER TO BRING ALONG
PICTURES • SOCIAL SECURITY # • AGENT'S PHONE

When you arrive at the casting office, LOOK for and READ the signs that tell you which Studio your commercial is being cast in. In casting offices when there are several studios – the Product name and Studio number is usually posted.

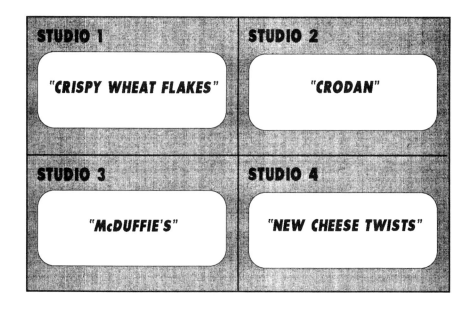

Then look for the SIGN–IN–SHEET
And make sure it's the correct one.   The product name is usually written on top.

(See example)

EXHIBIT E
SAG / AFTRA
COMMERCIAL AUDITION REPORT

THIS FORM MUST BE FILLED OUT IN INK

PAGE_____OF_____

COMMERCIAL PERFORMERS:
► Print your name.
► Print agent's name.
► Circle applicable interview.

TO BE COMPLETED BY CASTING DIRECTOR

(X) WHERE APPLICABLE

TELEVISION ☐   ON CAMERA ☐   OFF CAMERA ☐   RADIO ☐

AUDITION DATE

INTENDED USE   UNION: SAG ☐   AFTRA ☐   Person to whom correspondence concerning this form shall be sent:
(Name & Phone Number)

CASTING REPRESENTATIVE NAME   COMMERICAL TITLE - NAME & NUMBER   ADVERTISER NAME

PRODUCT   JOB NUMBER   ADVERTISING AGENCY AND CITY   PRODUCTION COMPANY

INSTRUCTIONS: Circle the name of performer hired if known.   Mail one copy to SAG OR AFTRA on the 1st and 15th of each month.

TO BE COMPLETED BY PERFORMERS

NAME (PLEASE PRINT)	SOCIAL SECURITY NUMBER	AGENT (PLEASE PRINT)	ACTUAL CALL	TIME IN	TIME OUT	INITIAL	CIRCLE INTERVIEW NUMBER	SEX (X)		AGE (X)		ETHNICITY (X)					PWD (X)
								M	F	+40	-40	AP	B	C	LH	I	
							1st 2nd 3rd 4th										
							1st 2nd 3rd 4th										
							1st 2nd 3rd 4th										
							1st 2nd 3rd 4th										
							1st 2nd 3rd 4th										
							1st 2nd 3rd 4th										
							1st 2nd 3rd 4th										
							1st 2nd 3rd 4th										
							1st 2nd 3rd 4th										
							1st 2nd 3rd 4th										
							1st 2nd 3rd 4th										
							1st 2nd 3rd 4th										
							1st 2nd 3rd 4th										
							1st 2nd 3rd 4th										
							1st 2nd 3rd 4th										

This recorded audition material will not be used as a client demo, an audience reaction commercial, for copy testing or as a scratch track without payment of the minimum compensation provided for in the Commercials Contract and shall be used solely to determine the suitability of the performer for a specific commercial.
AUTHORIZED
REPRESENTATIVE
SIGNATURE_____

The only reason for requesting information on ethnicity, sex, age, and disability is for the talent unions to monitor applicant flow. The furnishing of such information is on a VOLUNTARY basis. The Authorized Representative's signature on this form shall not constitute a verification of the information supplied by performers.

Asian/Pacific — AP   Latino/Hispanic — L
Black — B   Native American — I
Caucasian — C   Performer with Disability — PWD

2a EXE / 8

This is put out by the SAG Union and their main purpose is to keep track of how long you stayed at an audition. After an hour, you have to be compensated, and they can tell by this sheet.

Parents should fill these out for younger children but you who are old enough can do it yourself. Make sure you print <u>neatly</u> and <u>clearly</u> so that it can be easily read.

<u>Print</u> your name – Clearly, as it appears on your pictures. Parents be sure to print your child's name.

Social Security number – You should either have this with you or have it memorized.

Agent's name – Since this is a small space, try to print as much as you can but use initials if you have to.

Actual call – the time you were supposed to be there. This is time from which you would calculate your hours.

Time in – the time you actually arrived.

Time out – the time you finished your audition. Put this in AFTER THE AUDITION is over.

Initial – You can write your initials. You don't have to print.

Circle – The number of times you have been on that particular audition for that particular product. After the first time, you may have one, two or even three callbacks, but usually you only go twice before they cast it.

Sex – Check <u>M</u> (Male) or <u>F</u> (female)

(+40, –40) – Being a child you would of course check –40 years of age.

Ethnicity – Circle one of the race groups. The initials are explained at the bottom.

PWD – This spot is only for a Performer with Disability. Put an "X" here if you are disabled.

Then find out if they need a
SIZE SHEET
on which you write your contact information and measurements, etc. The size sheet is used by casting people and production companies for reference, call backs, matching up pairs, groups or families, and to get you the proper size wardrobe for the commercial if you get it. Unless the child is completely able and knows all the information, parents should fill these out.

It's important to know the correct, current sizes so that the right information is given and the correct sizes can be brought. Otherwise, a lot of time can be wasted and time is very precious and expensive during commercial productions.

Also be sure that your handwriting is neat and can be read easily. Here's an idea of what they look like and what information is needed.

Product_____　　**SIZE SHEET**

Date _____

Name _____

Home address _____

City_____ Zip_____

Home phone_____ Ans. service_____

Agent _____ Agent phone_____

age _____ weight_____ height_____ hair _____ eyes_____

Work Permit (if under 18 yrs.)　　☐ Yes ☐ No

measurements_____ ss# _____

suit_____ pants_____

jacket _____ dress_____ shirt/blouse_____

waist_____ inseam_____ shoes_____

hat_____ glove_____

SAG _____ AFTRA _____

```
┌──────────────────┐   Hobbies, special skills:
│                  │
│                  │   _____
│                  │
│     PHOTO        │   _____
│                  │
│                  │   _____
│                  │
│                  │   Will you work as an extra?
│                  │
└──────────────────┘       ☐ Yes    ☐ No
```

They come in all shapes and sizes and are sometimes called CASTING SHEETS. But the information needed is basically the same.

PRODUCT: Product name of the commercial you're being seen for.

DATE: Today's date

NAME: Your (the child's) name. If you have a professional name and it is different from your real name, put that as long as that is the name on your pictures.

AGENT: The name of your agency. Sometimes they want more than initials. If you have a commercial and theatrical agent, make sure you put your commercial agent.

UNIONS: Check the ones that you're a member of, if any. If you are not a member of any union, under 'Taft Hartley', you can do as many SAG commercials (union jobs) as you can get within 30 days. After 30 days, your very next SAG job, you must join and pay the fee which changes, so check with your SAG office.

NAMES OF UNIONS

SAG –   Screen Actors Guild

AFTRA– American Federation of Television and Radio Artists
          AFTRA is an open union. One year after joining AFTRA, you are eligible to join SAG.

Age: Children must give their real age because of child labor laws for different age groups.

Eyes: Your eye color.

Height: Since, as children, you are steadily growing, someone should measure you from time to time so you can give an accurate height.

Weight: The same goes for this. Weigh yourself often so you can be as close as possible. They need this information to get an idea of your body frame.

Hair: Hair color is especially important when they want a particular color or they're matching up families, groups or pairs. Hair length and texture are not necessary unless it's for a hair product and more information is needed. Take note though, to always let your agent know when you've changed your look by cutting your hair or changing your hair color.

Hands: Good, Fair or Bad. They need to know if your hands are in good enough condition to shoot up close.

Measurements:
          Know your current sizes since as children they change often. If you don't have some sizes like your glove or hat size, don't panic, just fill out what you can.

Inseam: The number of inches from the crotch to the point where your pants would end. This is not that crucial since most kids clothes are not measured by inseam, but just in case, look at the example below on how to measure it.

Hobbies / Special Skills:
          If you're involved in any sports activity, a particular hobby, or you have other skills like singing or dancing, list them in this section. One of them may be just what they're looking for. Be truthful though, so you won't be embarrassed or even hurt if you're asked to do something you really can't do.

Will you work as an extra?
          Extra work is good experience for beginners and it has happened that an extra player is upgraded to a <u>principal</u> and paid residuals. (It happened to me on a film). There are agencies that only deal with extras. These agents you can find in trade papers or in a drama bookstore. Be careful though, because you don't want your child to become known as only doing extra work , so talk to your agent about it.

     Well, that's the size sheet more or less except for the section for your polaroid.

• POLAROID

This space is for the polaroid snapshot which a casting person will take of you at the audition. They may ask you to stand against the wall and then from 2 or 3 feet away, they take a headshot that usually comes out looking pretty weird, but generally your are not cast from them and the picture is just used for a reference by the casting director and production company. Just make sure you give a nice natural smile unless you are asked to do something else like be serious (no smile) or give a big bright smile (almost laughing).

Parents, you can practice taking polaroids with your child at home. If you don't have a polaroid camera use a regular camera. Have the child stand against a wall and take several headshots at different levels of energy.

1. a nice natural smile
2. a very bright smile
3. a serious look

Do variations on each one and then review the pictures. If they look a little stiff and unnatural, try taking more. On auditions, they usually always take a polaroid so kids, the more comfortable you feel the better.

• COPY

After you fill out the size sheet find out if there is any COPY which is the dialogue for the commercial typed on a piece of paper. Examples of commercial copy will come later on in the chapter with our "practice commercials"

• STORYBOARDS

Sometimes STORYBOARDS are posted at the audition which is a series of drawings giving the story of what's going on in the commercial with the dialogue of each scene written underneath.
These give a good idea of :
– what each shot will be
– what you may be asked to do on your dialogue.
Sometimes they're a little hard to read and understand but look them over to get a general idea. (See example pg. 73).

WHILE WAITING – — BE QUIET

Usually there are auditions going on and waiting room noise is distracting so BE QUIET.

Parents 1. Bring quiet activities to keep kids busy.
              2. Bring a healthy no mess snack.
                 Watch out for food in the teeth.

Kids   1. Bring homework
              2. Work on copy.
              3. Limit socializing – If you see some friends, you can talk, but do it quietly and keep in mind the reason you're there.

• **LISTEN AND FOLLOW DIRECTIONS**

While you are waiting, a casting director or an assistant may come out and give you some directions on what you are to do in the audition room.

LISTEN CAREFULLY so that you can think about them and include them as you work on the copy.

If you haven't been told anything in the waiting area, when you get into the audition, you will be given directions so no matter what else is going on in the room, LISTEN and FOLLOW DIRECTIONS. (We will deal more with directions in our practice work on commercial copy later on in this chapter).

THE SLATE

The first thing they will ask you to do on camera is a slate which means to say your name on camera.

You will be asked to:

Stand on your mark – which is a specific spot on the floor marked with tape, like " T " or " ▬▬ ".

Wait for action cue – the casting director will signal you as to when you should begin. This gives them time to start the tape rolling so that you are recorded on camera.

State you name – You can say "Hi, my name is _____." Or just say your name.

And only if you're asked, give

Your age
    and
Agency

They may also ask you to do

Profiles – Which simply means to turn from side to side showing your right and left profile to camera.

Hands – You may be asked to hold up your hands so that they can see if they are in good condition in case you have to handle the product and your hands are shown on camera. It's a good idea to keep your hands and nails nice and clean and keep your nails clipped. Girls should not wear colored fingernail polish or false nails. The more natural looking the better.

So your Slate can include:

Name
Age
Agency
Profile
Hands

On your Slate you want to appear:
1. Confident
2. Relaxed
3. Pleasant to be around
4. The right person for the job

Practice at home. Set up a mock audition area with a mark on the floor. The "T" or " ▬▬ " is the center of the playing area. Directly across from you would be your camera and your mark on the wall like the ones on page 32.

Parents ask the child to stand in the mark, have them wait until you cue them, then ask them to say their

NAME – AGE – AGENCY

or

NAME – PROFILE – HANDS

or

NAME – PROFILE

or

NAME – HANDS

Mix the options up and practice until your child is :
1. Used to the procedures.
2. Can remember what they are supposed to say.
3. Feels comfortable and natural.

If you are using a video camera, playback what you've practiced. Kids, take a good look at yourself and make sure you
1. Speak loud enough and clear enough to be easily understood.
2. Have good posture.
3. Appeared confident, relaxed and a nice person to be around.

If you feel a little nervous, take a couple of deep breaths, remembering to exhale all the way and when you speak, use and speak from your diaphragm, the center of your energy, that we talked about in the warm-ups. This will give your voice more presence so it doesn't sound weak and nervous.

After the Slate comes the actual commercial that you will be auditioning for. There are all types so let's start with the simplest.

At auditions for commercials that have no dialogue and no particular action you may just take a polaroid, do a slate and then they may ask you to

- **TELL US SOMETHING ABOUT YOURSELF**

Which means they want you to talk a little bit on camera so that they can get a feeling about who you are, and the things you like to do.

Here are some things you can talk about:

1. Your family – How many kids in your family. How well you get along with your brothers and sisters,
   – the chores you do around the house.
2. School – What school you go to,
   – your favorite subjects,
   – what kind of grades you get,
   – other activities you're involved in at school.
3. Hobbies or Skills – sports that you're good at,
   – special activities or classes you're involved in,
   – different hobbies that interest you,
   – other abilities like: swimming, skating, bicycling, horseback riding, dancing, singing.
4. Places you've been – Trips that you've been on or that you are planning for the future.
5. Experience – Plays you have performed in, even school plays,
   – if you've done TV shows, movies or videos you can mention those.
   – **Don't** talk about a McDonald's commercial you did on a Burger King audition. Just say that you've done other commercials.

NOTE: Clients don't want to be able to identify you with another product. Besides, you are only allowed to have one commercial running at a time for a certain type of product, like one fast -food, one cereal, one soft drink, etc.

As far as talking about yourself, if you are a productive, active child, even if you have not had any professional experience, you should find plenty to say.

- **ONE-LINERS"**

At some auditions there may be commercial copy but it's only "one-line." I call these One-Liners. Now, even though you may only have to say ...

"IT'S GREAT!"

You as the performer, need to know <u>what</u> you are talking about and <u>really believe</u> that it's great!

Hopefully, you will be given some product information at the audition, at least the name of the product and what it is or what it does. You can even use a thought about something else that makes you feel the same way.

But on all your "one-liners" you need to figure out:
1. **What** you are talking about.
2. **How** you feel about it.

- **VISUALIZE**

It also helps to visualize or imagine the situation you are supposed to be in, whether eating a hamburger or at an amusement park or playing ball. The casting person may give you props to work with but for those things that you have to make-up, use your pantomime and mime techniques which we discussed in Chapter 1, and try to really visualize what you're talking about or reacting to.

- **PRACTICE ONE-LINERS**

Here are some examples of one liners that you can use for practice. Parents you can point to different ones or the child can choose. Create your product and situation and perform each one at different levels of energy and emotion. Play them directly to camera or use your mark on the wall. Also start some by using a SLATE first.

It's great!
No way
Um — delicious
I won! I won!
I'll take a double, double with cheese
I don't feel good

I don't believe it
No problem
It's just what I wanted
Ou - u ...
Ahh ...
I love it
How did you do that?
Not my fault
O - o - o, that's gross!
You're out!
Ooops, Sorry
I've gotta have some
Give me a break
This is so cool
Mom, my throat hurts
I can't wait
Is that it?
That's it

You can even make up some of your own. This is good exercise for expanding your performing ability, changing emotions quickly and using your creativity. Performing them at different levels helps to become more aware of making changes and adjustments in your performance. Quite often you may be asked to "bring the energy up some" or "tone it down."

• REACTIONS

At some auditions you may be asked to do a reaction with no words, just facial expression and body movements. To give the right expression you have to really <u>think the right thought</u> and feel the reaction, not just make it an external display. As with the one-liners, you should know
　– what you're reacting to
　– how you feel about it

Also VISUALIZE your situation and try to make it real for yourself. Perform at different levels of energy and emotion so that you can be more versatile.
These should be played to camera, or do your slate, then turn away from camera then back to camera with the reaction.

Remember just <u>THINK THE THOUGHT</u> , NO WORDS
WOW!
Which one will it be?
That's too funny
You scared me!
That's interesting
You must be kidding
I'm not so sure about that
Um — this is delicious
Looking good!
What happened
I don't feel so good
What a relief!
Please
Thank You

Work on getting a more expressive face and freer body language. As you change the intensity and the thought, the expression should also change.
BUT,
Make sure it's coming from within and you're not just making
faces.

• IMPROVISATION

I'm sure you've seen commercials where you <u>see</u> the people
moving and talking but you <u>don't hear</u> them. There's music or a
voice-over playing over it. On auditions for commercials like this
you may be asked to do 'improvisation' or 'improv'. You will most
likely be heard on the audition tape so you must make-up the
dialogue and action as you go along or improvise.
In improvising a situation you may also use the pantomime and
mime techniques and creative dialogue that we covered earlier.
Usually the casting director gives you a situation that you
create from.
For instance:

IMPROV 1: WATCHING A GAME
(Group)

There's a group of you at a baseball game cheering for the neighborhood team. During the improv I will call out different actions that are happening on the field like:

– the team coming out on the field
– they hit a home run
– it's a bad call
– your team wins

So I want you to change your actions accordingly. In between calls you can do cheers, order hot dogs, drinks, or just talk 'game talk.'

During the improv, while you're yelling, cheering and relating to the others, don't get so involved that you don't hear the directions being given. Stay aware so you can change your actions on cue.

• **GUIDES TO IMPROVS**

– Listen carefully to the directions being given to you and the other performers.
– Decide your relationship to the people you are working

with. This helps to make your actions more specific and honest.

– Visualize your space. Try to really imagine the area around you.

– Put the action or business in front of you so that you are playing to camera, unless you are directed otherwise.

– If specific actions or cues are given to you, perform them clearly, believably and in the time frame of the spot. *Don't take forever to get to the point.*

– Give & Take – This means you not only create and give your words and actions, <u>but</u> you also <u>listen</u> and react to the words and actions of the other performers. You give your input and you are open and receptive to take another's input.

– Relax and have fun – Make it a game for yourself. If you can't think of anything for the moment. Just relax, focus on the situation, making it as real as possible then let the creative juices flow.

Try these and then make up some of your own.

IMPROV 2: BREAKFAST
(Parent - Child)

It's morning and time for breakfast. Mom (or dad) has brought a new healthy type , low sugar cereal that she wants you to try. You would rather have your regular, sugar loaded cereal or nothing at all. Throughout the improv she tries to convince you that this cereal tastes just as good and is much better for you, while you make excuses like you're not that hungry – you have to get to school early and really don't have time to eat – or the other cereal has more prizes – whatever excuse you can think of not to try it.

Finally she gets you to taste a little and you immediately think that it's not quite as bad as you thought. Actually, you think it really tastes great and suddenly you're not in such a hurry and you pour a full bowl and eat it.

Remember to use the Guides to Improvs which we just covered.

IMPROV 3: SHOPPING
(Two friends)

You and a friend are shopping for an outfit for a party. You look through a few things that aren't quite right (For reasons that you should makeup, like it's the wrong color, not in style, it costs too much, etc.) Finally, you find the perfect outfit.
You can do it several ways:
– Shopping for one or the other person at a time,
– shopping for both together,
– shopping for someone else – a gift.
Parent – child: You can be shopping for a particular outfit for:
– Yourself (child)
– parent,
– someone else – a gift.

Use the "Guides to Improvs" and here again you look at several different things that don't work for reasons that you will create each time, until you find the perfect outfit and you are both satisfied.

IMPROV 4: WATCHING T.V.
(Single - group)

You're alone (or with someone else) are watching television, and what you are looking at causes you to change from one mood and emotion to another. For instance:
Interested
Mysterious
Happy
Anxious
Scared
Sad
Happy

This is a good exercise for a variety of emotions and you can also use creative dialogue. If you are alone, you're just responding to what is on T.V.,
making comments
laughing

sighing

crying

or whatever

Remember, your performance elements from Chapter One (page 29) to help make the exercise more real and natural. The transitions are very important and you should use your imagination and take your time to make them smooth and connect from one mood to another.

Parents: Cue them by calling out the reaction giving about 15 seconds for each change.

You can also add different ones that you create or even switch the order around for variety.

COMMERCIALS WITH DIALOGUE

Now let's move on to commercials with written dialogue or COPY. When you arrive at the audition, after you sign in, find out if there is copy available for you to read. If so, it will be on a plain piece of paper but in the audition room it may be on a Cue Card which we discussed in Part 1 Pg. 32.

Our first practice commercial is entitled "The Environment" and it is done by one person.

WIZARDS PRODUCTION GROUP

Client: Save the Earth
Job #:   Practice Spot #1
Title: "Environment"
Length: :15

You know everyone
this world belongs to all of us
and it's up to each one of us
to help preserve our natural resources.

Learn to recycle,
save water, plant trees
Do what you can do
to keep our world beautiful

• DIRECTIONS

The following are your directions in the scene, or blocking. To BLOCK a scene means to create and set your action within the scene.

This should be conversational but with a serious responsible tone. Play it directly into camera, as if you're talking to a friend or friends.

   — Sit in a comfortable yet attentive position on the first phrase. "You know ... all of us." i.e.: sitting facing the camera on a chair that is turned around backwards.
   — Rise slowly on the next phrase. "And it's up to ... natural resources."
   — Slowly walk around to the front of the chair while still speaking directly into camera on the next phrase. "Learn to recycle ... trees."
   — Stopping, facing camera, deliver the last phrase. "Do what ... world beautiful."

Remember the camera is 'a person' who you're speaking to or a group of people on a 'one to one' level. So think of the camera not just as a piece of machinery, but as 'a person', a buddy or girlfriend that you're 'kicking it' with.

Use a white poster board to copy the commercial on. Write clearly and large enough to be seen across the room.

For most of the practice spots all you'll need is a couple of chairs and a table. You can substitute for props or be creative and make some. For this spot all you need is a chair.

To get a good understanding about the commercial, let's do our copy breakdown as we did in Part 1 (Pg. 28). Be aware, though, that at an audition there isn't much time, so your copy breakdown would be a quick mental process.

But for practice and so that you can get used to doing it in your head quickly, let's do one on the "Environment."

1. What is the Overall Thought?

We are all responsible to help save the environment.

2. What do they want us to think or feel (about the product)?

There is no product per say, but they want you and the audience to feel like what happens in your environment is up to you and we can all do positive things that can help to save it.

3. What are the descriptive words or phrases?

Now, I know that 'adjectives' are descriptive words but in commercials there may be adjectives or phrases that describe the product or just catch phrases that they want the audience to remember.

So with this in mind, let's look at some descriptive words and phrases or 'catch' phrases in 'The Environment.' (Actually this one is full of "catch" phrases, so let's underline a few).

You know everyone
this world <u>belongs to all of us</u>
and <u>it is up to **each** one of us</u>
to help <u>preserve our **natural** resources</u>

<u>Learn to recycle</u>
<u>Save water, plant trees</u>
Do what you can do to
<u>keep our world **beautiful**.</u>

The descriptive <u>words</u> are bold underlined but as you can see, there are many phrases.

4. Are there any changes in thought or emotion – Transitions?
There is a small transition or change in thought between the first part and the second part.

1st PART:

You know everybody ...

... preserve our natural resources

You are making the audience aware of their responsibility to the environment.

2nd PART:

Learn to recycle ...

... keep our world beautiful.

You are giving positive suggestions on what they can do to help.

5. Are there any comparisons or objections?
There are some comparisons that you can assume are being made like:

recycle materials – – as opposed to – – creating waste
save water – – as opposed to – – wasting water
plant trees – – as opposed to – – destroying them

6. What are the benefits?
Everyone benefits by having and keeping the world beautiful.

Doing copy breakdowns like this should really help to add more meaning to your delivery.

MORE WORK ON COPY

As you read through it, add your <u>Performance Elements</u> as we discussed in Part 1 Pg. 29.

1. Concentration – Stayed Focused

2. Articulation – Give us the words.

3. Creative Expression – Be expressive.
    In this commercial you're relating the seriousness of one's responsibility. Believe in what you're saying. Practice it several ways. From very serious to light and friendly.

4. Spontaneity – Let it happen.
    Even though, in this commercial, many of the phrases have been heard before and in practicing, as in any commercial you repeat over and over, make each time fresh, spontaneous, with genuine sincerity.

5. Transitions – make the change in thought that we talked about in the copy breakdown – <u>clearly</u> and <u>smoothly</u>.

• **DELIVERY TECHNIQUE**

Practice your delivery technique that we discussed in Part 1 Pg. 31.
Using the cue card or the written copy, quickly read a phrase or sentence at a time then focus back into camera or a mark on wall.

• **MEMORIZATION** (Pg. 30)

This comes with repetition and working out trouble spots.

• **TIME**

Notice that the time, the length of the commercial, is :15 seconds. Get a stop watch and practice doing the spot with all the directions and performance elements within :15 seconds.
In a :15 second spot, your actual speaking time may only be

13 - 14 seconds so practice shaving off seconds. Don't just start talking faster. Try to pull your phrases together as you speak with a little more crispness and energy.

At the actual audition, after you've worked in the copy and memorized it, then relax. If it is a long wait be sure to go back to the copy now and then to stay fresh.

WIZARDS PRODUCTION GROUP

Client: Natural Grape Juice
Job #:   Practice Spot #2
Title: "It's a Natural!"
Length: :30 seconds

You know what this grape juice is
made out of?

Grape juice, that's it!
Pure, simple, delicious grape juice.

No added flavors, no added colors,
not even added sugar.

But it's sweet enough
because the grapes they use are just ripe
enough.

And when it goes down (take a drink)
it hits the spot every time!

Then for an encore
you get this burst of grape flavor
all in your mouth.

I'm telling you, it's a Natural!

To get used to **putting it all together**, in working on this copy, we're going to put the points in the copy breakdown and the performance elements into the directions.

Directions:
The **tone** of this commercial is conversational.
(You will hear this term often. *'The tone of the commercial'*)
So like I said it's conversational, as if you're talking to a buddy. You want us to know that
  − You appreciate the natural quality of this grape juice,
  − you enjoy the taste, and
  − you're passing along this great bit of information that everyone should know about and enjoy too.

Play directly into camera, seated at a table with the bottle of grape juice and an empty glass.
Your main focus or overall thought is that this grape juice is good, it's sweet and it comes that way naturally with nothing added.
The storyboard on the following page not only gives you the dialogue but also your action and an idea of what the shots will be.

You know what this grape juice is made of?

Grape juice, that's it!

Pure, simple, delicious grape juice.

No added flavors, no added colors, not even added sugar.

But it's sweet enough.

Because the grapes they use are just ripe enough.

And when it goes down...

It hits the spot everytime!

Then for an encore, you get this burst of grape flavor all in your mouth.

I'm telling you, it's a Natural!

– On the first line, a question, push the grape juice straight to camera. You know what this grape juice ...? You are asking your friend, who may be drinking something with a lot of junk in it, if he or she is aware of how pure this grape juice is.

– On the next two lines, "Grape juice ... that's it. Pure ... grape juice.," You're pouring a glass of juice and speaking directly to camera in a very matter of fact way. You are simply stating, in a pleasant, straight forward manner, the qualities of the juice.

– On "No flavoring ... not even added sugar", point to the ingredients with the right hand. This is also matter-of-fact and when you get to "Not even added sugar," it should be said like everybody knows that most drinks have added sugar at least, but this grape juice doesn't even have that.

– "But it's sweet enough ... ripe enough", will be voice over so just speak directly to camera with a bright smile.

– After you say "when it goes down", take a nice drink, savor it, really taste it as it goes down (use pantomime here too, or real juice).

– As you put the glass down and enjoy the drink you just had say "it hits the spot every time."

– Then still experiencing a mouth full of delicious grape flavor from the one drink that you took say, "Then for an encore ... in your mouth."

– The last line move the bottle under your chin and rest your hands and chin on top of the bottle as you say,

"I'm telling you, it's a natural!"

Attitude on last line

– take my word for it, it says natural, it is natural.

– there's no question about it

– it's just as natural and wonderful as I am.

Also put this commercial on a Cue Card and practice your delivery technique.

Some of the performance elements were in the directions, but review them to make sure you're getting the most out of your work.

• TIMING

Now using a stopwatch, time yourself and work on doing the spot between :25 - 28 seconds, making it a second or two longer or shorter just to get used to "shaving off seconds" or "stretching it out."

WIZARDS PRODUCTION GROUP

Client: Children's Formula 4
Job #:   Practice Spot #3
Title: "Feeling Better"
Length: :30 seconds

Mom and child at kitchen counter. Formula 4 in background. Mom finishes wrapping child up in outdoor clothes, gives him/her a kiss. *Child turns to camera.*	CHILD: My mom takes good care of me.
Child reaches for children's Formula 4	You see, when I had this really bad cold, she gave me Children's Formula 4
Putting it back	She says doctor prescribe it most.
Child starts to gather up lunch box and backpack to leave for school.	Well, they should because it sure made me feel better.
Close up of product	V.O.: I'm glad she told them about it. Announcer V.O.: Children's Formula 4. Doctor's prescribe it most.

The tone of this commercial is very sweet and warm.

You, as the child, have just recovered from a bad cold because your mom, who always takes good care of you, has given you Children's Formula 4. You're glad you're feeling better and back to normal.

The directions are written on the left side of the copy that coincide (or goes along with) the dialogue on the right. This kind of copy gives you more information as to what's going on in the spot so read both sides carefully, even though during an actual shooting anything can change.

As you read through it do a copy breakdown.
- decide overall thought,
- how you feel about the product,
- descriptive words
- transitions
- comparisons
- benefits of taking the product.

Remember your performance elements and use what applies to this spot.

Concentration
Articulation
Creative Expression
Spontaneity
Transition

The spot is :30 seconds with not much dialogue so you can take your time and really act it out.

• ADDITIONAL DIRECTIONS

- Show affection for your mom.
- Let us know that you were really feeling bad until your mom gave you this medicine.
- Tell us how this is the medicine that doctors choose most and they should because it worked for you and now you can go back to school.
- On your last line, "I'm glad mom told them about it," you're being naive but innocently. You really think that your mom was the one who discovered Children's Formula 4 and was nice enough to tell the doctors about it. Even though it's a voice over (V.O.), you still need to have the thought behind the line.

—   While the announcer says his or her line (also a V.O.), you can be saying good-bye to your mom and leaving the house.

It would be good to work with props like jacket, scarf, lunch box, backpack and medicine bottle. Follow the directions on the left and time your actions to fit the lines but be sure you're playing it all towards camera.

WIZARDS PRODUCTION GROUP

Client:　Roll-Up Bar
Job#:　　Practice Spot #4
Title:　　"Delicious & Nutritious"
Length:　:30 seconds

If you're feeling kind of listless
and you want something delicious
kind of fruity and nutritious
just to satisfy your wishes

Try the super fruity
double - licious
richest yet nutritious – –
a fruity rootie, rootin-tootie Roll-Up
Bar!

Do a quick copy breakdown:

– Your overall thought and feeling – – the "Roll-Up Bar" is a delicious, nutritious, fun to eat snack that can brighten your day.

– Descriptive words, there are plenty of those, some unfamiliar so using your performance elements, work through them making each one clear, different, special.

– Transitions — each line, especially in the first part, has a different thought behind it but all connected. Therefore, you need to make soft, subtle but definite transitions between them.

• PERFORMANCE ELEMENTS

All of the elements apply here especially <u>articulation</u> and <u>creative expression</u> which means you have to focus. In order for each performance to be fresh, you must be <u>spontaneous,</u> and we've already discussed the <u>transitions.</u>

The tone of this commercial is upbeat and rhythmic. There is a definite beat, 'rap style,' that should go on throughout the spot with lots of fun.

Play it straight to camera and you can even make up dance movements to go with it. The actual filming of the spot may be a series of different scenes or "cuts", but for practice you should do the entire spot to camera.

Remember to pronounce the words clearly, keep it moving in the rhythm and let it build toward the end.

WIZARDS PRODUCTION GROUP

Client: Wizard Toy Co.
Job#:   Practice Spot #5
Title: Robi
Length: :30 seconds

Wow! Look at Robi

She's so tall and pretty

With long, beautiful hair
(or - short, curly hair)

that I can style just like mine

and she has all the latest fashions

just like me!

I'm into Robi

Review your performance elements and do a quick copy breakdown.

• **DIRECTIONS**

The tone of this commercial spot is bright, and excited. You love playing with dolls. You're fascinated with Robi because you imagine that you look just like her, including the hair.

(Change the words in the lines about her hair to fit your style of hair).

You and Robi dress in the same styles and may have on the same outfit.

In your delivery:
– Keep your interest and energy high,
– make your choices definite,
– make each one of the things you like about her different and special.

You can be sitting,holding her up on the table on the first two lines.

The next two lines will probably be a tight shot of you styling her hair.

"With long beautiful hair ...

... just like mine.

So for this practice audition you can touch her hair and act like you're finishing up a style.

Then on the next line

"And she's got all the latest fashions, ... just like me" set her down on the table, stand up and pose in front of an imaginary mirror. In the actual shoot, you and Robi would have the same outfit and pose.

Then pick her up and very positively, convincingly, and full of excitement about her, say the last line, "I'm into Robi!"

WIZARDS PRODUCTION GROUP

Client: Wizard Toy Co.
Job #:   Practice Spot #6
Title: "Crodan, Be Ready!"
Length: :30 seconds

If you mess with Crodan

You better be ready.

Because he's got the power,

the moves,

And the raw muscle

to wipe out any opponent.

So if you're even thinking about

challenging Crodan,

You better be ready! Raahh!!

You should be doing a copy breakdown mentally by now and adding the performance elements as you go. For a review of the format and terms refer to page 28–29.

The tone of this spot is high energy, very strong, powerful and threatening. This spot is about a superhero that you think is the toughest one out there. (overall thought). He's strong and powerful and can do devastating karate moves.

In your delivery we have to feel the strength and be threatened by the power of Crodan.

Throughout the spot you should demonstrate Crodan's power and moves by imitating him. Of course you have to create the moves yourself.

• DIRECTIONS

– On the first line strike the Crodan stance. "If you mess with Crodan you better be ready."

– Then on "Because he's got the power ... , on the word "power" do a power move.

– "the moves ...", do a side kick or spin kick for example.

– "And the raw muscle..." show us your muscles.

– Then do an arm move on "... to wipe out any enemy."

– Then with a real threatening look, like the wrestlers, say "... so if you even think about challenging Crodan..."

– Pick the Crodan figure up and push it toward camera on " ... You better be ready."

– Then put the figure close to your face on " ... RAAAH!"

COMMERCIALS WITH 2 OR MORE PEOPLE

If two or more kids are available – fine. If not, parent or instructor, you can say the line off camera and the child plays directly to camera which is what happens in an audition some-times.

WIZARDS PRODUCTION GROUP

Client: Wizards Cereals
Job #:   Practice Spot #7
Title: Crispy Wheat Flakes – "Too Healthy"
Time: :30 seconds

A child is sitting and enjoying breakfast.	KID 1: Hey, whatcha eatin?
Friend (Kid 1) enters and sits next to child (Kid 2). *(Bowl and cereal are on the table)*	
Kid 2 offers him some.	KID 2: They're called Crispy Wheat Flakes, want some?
Kid 1 refuses, a little disappointed because he is hungry but these don't seem too appetizing.	KID 1: No thanks, they sound too healthy.
Kid 2 explains that they still taste good and they're good for you.	KID 2: They are healthy but they're also good. They even have a touch of honey.
Kid 1 figures they might not be too bad so he tries some and is surprised that he really likes them.	KID 1: Let me try 'em ... (eats) Umm, delicious ... I like these.
Kid 2 teases Kid 1 reminding him of what he said earlier.	KID 2: I thought you said they were too healthy.
They both agree and slap high fives that they're not "Too Healthy", they're good!	BOTH: NOT!!

This one can be done by any combination, even though in the directions, both were referred to as "he."

2 boys	boy – girl
2 girls	girl – boy

and switch roles so you experience both parts. It's always good to learn <u>both</u> parts so that:
- you know what to react to
- you can pick up your cues
- you can switch roles if you're asked to.

At the actual audition when it involves more than one person always try to find out who you will be reading with and practice with them. Usually a casting director will assign you to a partner or group so be aware. If it's crowded, it may take a while but you can always politely ask the casting director or an assistant.

The directions for this are written on the copy so read them carefully. As far as your position goes, make sure you are turned toward the camera. Do your copy breakdown Pg.28 and add your performance elements Pg. 29. Be sure to pick up your cues and keep it moving even though there may be extra time. That time will be for product shots, so pick up your cues.

WIZARDS PRODUCTION GROUP

Client: Grainola Bars
Job#:   Practice Spot #8
Title: "Call it a Cookie"
Length: :30 seconds

#1: (Sitting and enjoying a Grainola Bar)

#2: (Entering, thinking he / she has
      caught the older one)
          Oooo. You're eating a cookie.

#1: No I'm not. This is a Grainola Bar.

#2: Uh - oh. That's not good for you.

#1: Yes it is. It's full of grains and oats.

#2: That's a cookie!

#1: No it's not. It's a nutritious snack
      that really tastes good. And mom
      says ...

#2: Okay, I'll try it. (tastes it and likes it)
      Ummm. This is a Grain-e-o-ly bar?
      (mispronouncing it)

#1: Just call it a cookie.

Kid #1 should be older.
Kid #2 younger.

Can be brothers, sisters, or sister / brother. The tone of this spot is very real and natural. Really focus on what you are doing and saying so that you can <u>pick up your cues</u> and keep the spot moving, making it sound natural and conversational with energy and personality. Pay attention to punctuation, use lots of <u>creative expression</u>, and have fun with it.

• DIRECTIONS

   — Throughout the spot make sure you angle yourself toward the camera.

   — Kid 2, thinking he's caught Kid 1 doing something wrong and doesn't want to get in trouble, until Kid #1 convinces him it's nutritious.

   — Kid #1 is just trying to be patient and explain.

   — Another way to play it is Kid #1 is more of a know-it-all and thinks #2 is silly and doesn't understand anything.

If you're using an actual snack bar just take little, tiny bites that look like big bites so that you will be able to do the dialogue without choking or spitting the food out.

WIZARDS PRODUCTION GROUP

Client: Wizards Toys
Job #:   Practice Spot #9
Title: Dinomite
Length: :30 seconds

Kid 2 watching TV, bored,

KID 1: Hey, you wanna play a great new game?!

Kid 1 enters, excited.

Not wanting to be bothered.

KID 2: I don't want to play any silly little game.

Opening and setting up the game to play.

KID 1: It's not a silly game. It's called Dinomite and it has lots of dinosaurs and amazing adventures.

Becoming interested, examining it. Then his interest grows to excitement about playing.

KID 2: Let me see ... Hmmm ... Tyrannosaurus Rex, the Saber-toothed Tiger, Brontosaurus, hidden caves, mud swamps! ... I'll try it! How do you play?

Kid 1 continues the dialogue, ad-libbing, explaining the game to Kid 2. Then there is a montage of them playing the game; taking turns rolling the dice and moving the pieces, Kid 1 getting ahead, then Kid 2, Each react anxiously to hitting a trouble spot, then playing different emotions: tension, surprise, etc. Then Kid 2 wins.

KID 1: Okay, this is how it goes ...

KID 1: Hey I didn't say you could win.

KID 2: You're a great teacher. But to beat me, you have to be Dinomite!

WIZARDS PRODUCTION GROUP

Client: Wizards Toys
Job #:   Practice Spot #9
Title: Dinomite
Length: :30 seconds

ALTERNATE ENDING *Kid 1 wins!*	KID 2: Hey, you won! KID 1: That's right. To beat me you have to be Dinomite!

The spot can be done by any combinations of boy and girls. Kid1 may be a little younger than Kid 2.

The tone is excitement and adventure. At first Kid 2 is not at all interested until Kid 1 shows him what Dinomite is all about, then the fun, excitement and adventure begin. Kid 2 – as you're examining the game and getting excited, make sure it starts low and then builds gradually with each discovery, until you get totally into it and enthusiastic about wanting to play.

Work on the pronunciation of the dinosaurs names until you can say them easily.

There's room for lots of creative expression and spontaneity, so have fun with it and let us believe that the game is taking you on an adventure.

The directions are written on the copy and they include improvisation.

Parents or instructors, you should give the directions during the 'montage.'

For instance:
– Kid 1, it's your turn,
– Okay, Kid 2, it's your turn,
– Kid 1 is ahead
– Kid 2 is ahead
– One of them gets in trouble in the mud swamp, etc.

After you practiced the whole spot one way, then do the alternate ending where Kid 1 wins.

WIZARDS PRODUCTION GROUP

Client: Wizard Computer
Job #:   Practice #10
Title: New Computer
Length: :30 seconds

CHILD: (enthusiastically working with her brand new computer system)

MOM: (enters) Hey baby, you like your new computer?

CHILD: Yeah mom, it's great!

MOM: Need any help?

CHILD: Nope, the computer gives me all the help I need.

MOM: (Looking for a way to help) How about your homework? I know you need some help with that.

CHILD: Nope, I'll just work it out on the computer.

MOM: (Feeling a little left out) Nice computer huh?

CHILD: Yeah, it's great, thanks.

MOM: (Trying anything to get her away from the computer) You wanna go shopping?

CHILD: No ... I ...

MOM: (Giving up) I know, you wanna work on your computer.

CHILD: Yeah!

Parent and child can do this together. You can also do a copy breakdown and review your performance elements. Here are some directions with a little bit of both.

- **DIRECTIONS**

Child: (Let's say it's a girl) As written in the copy, on the opening you have gotten a brand new computer and you are completely engrossed in it. When your mom starts talking to you, you answer her but she doesn't really have your full attention because you are into that computer. You're even enjoying doing your homework because the computer is so much fun and a great help. Even shopping, which is your favorite thing, doesn't tempt you.

For a moment, you're "kinda" sorry because you know your mom wants to spend time with you but right now your new computer is #1.

Parent: You've made a big investment and you feel like it is a good one and the best thing for your child right now, so in the beginning you're sincerely happy that she's working on it and enjoying it, although you kind of miss her company.

You think you may get in there when you ask about helping with the homework, but to your surprise and a little dismay, she doesn't need your help there either. You decide to play dirty and tempt her with 'shopping.' You just know that'll get her. But it doesn't so you "throw in your hand' and decide to 'lie in the bed you made.' In other words, you give up nobly and realize that you bought the computer hoping that he / she would be interested in it and enjoy using it. So you got what you asked for and that's Okay.

WIZARDS PRODUCTION GROUP

Client: Wizards Fast Foods
Job#:   Practice Spot #11
Title: McDuffie's
Length: :30 seconds

3 Kids, brothers and sisters (any combination) are waiting anxiously for the 4th brother / sister to bring mom's surprise birthday breakfast.	
Then finally, he / she comes in.	KID 1: Did you get it?
	KID 2: Did you get something?
Entering with McDuffie's bag.	KID 3: Yep, I got an egg and cheese biscuit, hash browns, orange juice and coffee. I even got us some pancakes.
Yelling out	KID 4: Yeah! Pancakes!
All the other kids quiet kid #4	KID 1, 2, 3: S-h-h-h-h!
	KID 2: Did we have enough money?
	KID 1: You must be kidding
	KID 3: We sure did. We even had some change left.
Yelling Out	KID 4: Alright!

Practice Spot #11 — (Continue next page)

WIZARDS PRODUCTION GROUP

Client: Wizards Fast Foods
Job#:   Practice Spot #11 — (Continued)
Title: McDuffie's
Length: :30 seconds

The kids quiet him / her down again.	KID 1, 2,3: S-h-h-h-!
They all whisper together and tip toe to mom's room.	ALL: LET'S GO
As they present the breakfast with pride to a surprised MOM.	ALL: HAPPY BIRTHDAY MOM!

As it says in the directions on the copy (so read carefully) this is a family of 4 kids. It can be any combination and you should switch roles.

It's mom's birthday and you have all put your money together to buy her breakfast from McDuffie's, your favorite place to eat.

You are all waiting anxiously, improvising dialogue
- hoping mom doesn't wake up,
- hoping everything is okay,
- wishing Kid 3 would hurry back,
- wondering if he got the right thing.

These are a few 'seeds for thought' but don't make the improv and *ad libs* too long. You should only talk for about 4 *beats* (4 seconds). And then Kid 3 enters.

Kid 3 has gone to the store and has gotten the McDuffie's Breakfast Special and splurged a little on pancakes for you guys.

You all turn to him and the first two lines come very quickly, right on top of each other. So Kid 2 has to pick up the cue right away. You don't want to wake up mom so don't talk too loud, but do speak up.

KID 1: You're the doubter. You always think that things aren't going to turn out as well as they do, but you're a good kid and you want them to work but you doubt they will.

KID 2: More optimistic and enthusiastic about the whole idea. Even though you asked questions, they're in a positive 'expecting the good' tone.

KID 3: The oldest, you are very proud of your purchase. Make sure you work on the list of things you brought so that you say them correctly and in the right order. You're also proud and happy that you have change left.

KID 4: Probably the youngest and loudest. You know how the baby of the family is. "Big Mouth." You just can't hold back. Pancakes are your favorite, but after they S-h-h-h you, you quiet down until you hear that there's some money leftover and there goes that big mouth again. But again, don't keep it going, you quiet down. And quietly tip toe to mom's room.

The three of you kids 1, 2, 4 are standing together in the beginning and make sure you angle your bodies towards camera and the same goes for Kid 3 who enters. Don't talk with your body sideways, (facing the other kids) turn more toward camera.

When you all decide to go to mom's room, for audition purposes just tip-toe around in a circle, in your individual spot but all at the same time in the same direction, then by the time you are all facing the camera again, you have reached mom's room. Then all together, in a nice, loud, happy voice say "Happy Birthday Mom." Hold a couple of beats with nice bright smiles, until your parent or instructor says "cut."

WIZARDS PRODUCTION GROUP

Client: Wizards Snacks
Job #:   Practice Spot #12
Title: New Cheese Twists
Length: :15 seconds

#1	#1	#1	New Cheese Twists have a whole lot of snap!
#2	#2	#2	And a great new cheesy taste!
#3	#1	#3	I can eat a whole bunch!
#4	#2	#1	Even put 'em in my lunch!
#5	#1	#2	They can go anyplace!

The numbers on the side represent the different parts. First, practice the whole commercial as one. Then play a different part each time, coming in on cue, so that you get used to listening to other parts and picking up your cues on time.

      Example: First time you do the whole thing.
               Next time through you only do #1
               Next time through you do #2, etc.

Parents or instructors, I've just given you three combinations. You can switch the parts around and make up your own combinations, but use another piece of paper or cue card to write the commercial down with one number in front of each line so that the child can see it clearly. Then do it again changing numbers. Have the child play directly to camera, and you read the other lines off camera as a casting director would do.

• DIRECTIONS

Kids, here are some suggestions for direction on each line. For props, use any kind of cheese puffs, pretzel, chips, etc.

"New Cheese Twists have a whole lot of snap."
– You take one out on "New Cheese Twists", then break it in half after " ... snap".
– or you take one out on "New Cheese Twists", then eat it and say "has a whole lot of snap", snaps your fingers on the word snap.

"And a great new cheesy taste."
– eats one before saying the line.
– point to a 'new' sign on the package.

"I can eat a whole bunch."
– pouring them in a bowl while saying the line.
– or spreading arms out wide while saying the line.
– or hugging a big bowl full while saying the line.

"Even put 'em in my lunch."
– putting a pack in your lunch box while saying line.
– or taking a pack out of your lunch box while saying line.

Or use alternate line

"Even put 'em in your lunch."
– You take a pack out of someone else's lunch pail.

"They can go anyplace."
– putting a pack in your gym bag.
– putting a pack in your jacket pocket.
– hiding a pack under your pillow.
– hiding a pack in your desk.

You can use these directions or make up your own, but as the direction changes, so should your attitude and how you say the line.

This can also be done by a group of kids as a rap song and dance. You can have some fun making up your own moves to go with the words but make sure you play it to camera.

CHAPTER WRAP UP

Alright, we've gone over a dozen practice commercials and you can always find more
- in magazines or newspaper
- make up some of your own
- copy some from TV
- as you audition, write down the copy to practice at home.

Get in the habit of doing a **copy breakdown** even if it's done mentally, so that you have an idea of what you're thinking in the commercial and where the changes come.

Remember your performance elements so that your delivery is
- clear and articulate
- believable and full of expression
- spontaneous and fresh each time you do it.
- focused. If you stay focused, you're more able to do the correct moves and dialogue and think the right thoughts.

Once you begin the audition process treat each one as a learning experience so that the more you go on, the better you'll get.

GENERAL TIPS FOR AUDITIONS

• **BE PROFESSIONAL**

Keep a professional attitude out in the waiting area and in the audition room. Too much noise in the waiting area can really be distracting to the filming going on inside and can put you on the wrong side of the casting director.

Even in the audition room, be careful about fooling around and cracking jokes about the product. The clients usually don't think that's funny. So be quiet, remember why you are there and be professional.

• DEALING WITH THE PRESSURE

Learning to relax, listen, and focus is a big part of your audition technique. Relaxation helps you to stay open and let all your other work show through. Listening and focusing helps keep your attention on your main objective.

It always pays to mentally review your auditions, even the good ones, because obviously in those you made some good choices. Saying "I should have" is not as constructive as saying "I could have" which leads to more positive statements like, "I could have done it this way, so next time in a similar situation I'll be more relaxed and focused and I'll make the better choice or perform better."

If you decide to get depressed and worry about not getting a job, not only does it make you feel bad, but you can carry it over to the next audition. "Oh, I don't know why I'm bothering, I'm not going to get it anyway." Not a good attitude, and a complete waste of time and effort. Love yourself. Be kind to yourself. Tell yourself you did a good job, you did your best. Or if you didn't do your best, review why and work on that.

If you really work on yourself and practice your techniques, when you **do** get a job, you'll be ready.

Your turn will come, keep the faith!

Chapter 3

How To

Keep Doing

Them

In this chapter we will discuss doing the job and doing it right. Now before you actually book a job several other things might happen.

THE CALLBACK

Most commercials require a callback (2nd audition) before it is cast. The first call is usually run by the casting director and the callback is run by the director of the commercial, and is also attended by the clients. Some commercials even have a second callback, for which you get paid under union rules. Try to keep your copy in case you do get a callback. If you can't keep it, *(and most casting directors don't want you to take them)* jot the words down right afterwards while the commercial is still fresh in your mind.

REVIEWING: In reviewing and working on a spot for your callback, don't change it too much from your first audition. Just clean it up, practice until you know it well and it flows. Also, practice it with slight attitude changes because often on callbacks a director will ask you to shade your performance one way or another, or ask you to make it more real and simple. Knowing it well doesn't mean it will be stale, but should help you to make the words your own and say them without thinking about them.

CHANGES: Always be prepared for changes in dialogue and action on callbacks. Although you may have worked on the copy, you may have to do something totally different and be expected to perform it just as well. This is the nature of the business. So always get to a callback in enough time to get and work on any changes. Ask the casting director questions such as:

–Do they want the same thing?
–Am I reading for the same part?

Sometimes they don't know and when you get in the audition room, things may still change.

LISTEN TO THE DIRECTIONS FIRST MAKING SURE YOU HEAR AND UNDERSTAND ALL OF THEM.

If you have any questions, ask them. But make sure you really have to have something explained and you're not asking to be asking. Be careful of sticking your opinion into it even though commercials are sometimes a little silly, unnatural or "off the wall."

Just try to do what you're asked to do and don't let negative thinking or attitudes get in the way of making the material sound natural and believable.

Commercials using reactions or improv are also subject to change, like different cues or timing on reactions. So again, listen carefully to the directions given and ask a question if you don't understand. Other than that, just focus and have fun!

If there is a 2nd callback (3rd audition), my notes are the same.
1. Work on your material.
2. Pay attention to directions.
3. Listen for changes and adjust.
4. Focus and have fun.

• WARDROBE ON CALLBACK

As far as wardrobe is concerned, it doesn't hurt to wear the same thing you had on in the first call, or at least something very similar, unless you're told otherwise by your agent.

• 'ON AVAIL'

If the client is interested in you but they haven't quite made up their minds your agent may call and tell you that you're – 'On Avail', which means that the clients and the director have not made up their minds yet but they are interested in you and they're checking to see if you are available to work on a certain day or days. Always keep your agent posted on any changes in your availability so that they can let the CD know immediately and try to work things out.

Sometimes you may be 'on avail' and you still don't get the job. Not much fun. They decide to go with someone else. No problem, just move on. At least, you find out in enough time so if you get another job, you can take it.

• BOOKED THE JOB

This means that you have been chosen to do the job and are set to work on a certain day or days. YES!

Booking the job is one thing, doing it is a "whole 'nother ball game."

When you do book a job you would want it to go well. You want to be professional and have your performance be at it's best.

Directors and clients remember the good ones, as well as, the "never agains". It's important to establish a good rep so casting directors will want to call you again and directors will want to work with you again.

Getting the job is one feat accomplished, but by no means is your work completed. Doing the job is another. The actual shooting is the one for the money, the time to really shine. This is your pay–off, but like running a race, the last stretch can be the hardest.

Here are some things you should know to help you to do well and better your chances of getting more commercials.

- **BE PHYSICALLY READY**

You need to be healthy, in good shape and well rested because the hours are often long and tedious, and the lights very hot.

If you're one who likes to stay up watching TV half the night, forget it. Go to sleep and get your rest. You'll need it because you'll probably have to get up early, have a long day and you don't want to 'poop–out' on the set.

THE WARDROBE CALL

This call is usually a couple of days before your shoot day and here is where they decide what you will wear in the commercial.

I underline 'they' because it is their decision, not yours. Sometimes they will ask you if you like a certain outfit and hopefully the one they pick, you will like, but the final decision is theirs.

On the wardrobe call, you'll probably be asked to bring a whole bunch of your own clothes. If they pick something that you've brought then they'll pay you for the use of it so mark it on your contract. The wardrobe person may have also done some shopping for you. They get your sizes from the SIZE SHEET you filled out at the casting session or audition. That is why it's so important to know and put down your correct sizes on the SIZE SHEET.

Whatever outfit you end up wearing, remember just go along with the program and be professional.

THE SHOOT

We already talked about being professional at the audition and it's most important during the shooting of the commercial. Here are some pointers. Parents take note.

1. Know the correct date or dates that you work and mark them in your datebook. If it's a weather permit call, which means they'll shoot if the weather is suitable, you may end up shooting on that date or the day or days following that date.

2. Know exactly where the commercial is being shot. If it's a sound stage – know the address of the lot and the number of the stage. i.e. Stage 1, Stage 2, etc.

If it's being shot on location, get a map and/or directions which you already understand before the day you shoot. Usually they are given to you at the wardrobe call. When you receive them, read through them right away and clear up any questions you may have.

3. Know your copy. You need to know your copy inside out and be able to add or take off seconds. Even though they still may change the dialogue, know it well enough so that you can do it without thinking about it.

4. Bring the Work Permit. A child cannot work without it. You give the work permit to the social worker on the set so they can check and make sure it's up to date, mark the job on the back of it and return it to you.

5. Bring School Work. When school is in session, school work must be done on the set, during designated times with a teacher / social worker. If school is out just bring something to read or quiet, still games. Often times the teacher / social worker has something for you to do. If you are working with other actors try to watch them (staying quiet and out of the way), to learn what to do and <u>not</u> to do.

6. **Prepare for your comfort on the set.** I have frozen my buns off doing a summer shot when the weather was more like winter. Parents, come prepared, you and your kids are going to be out in the elements so bring along extra undergarments or cut off long johns that'll fit under the wardrobe.

If you anticipate that the ground may be damp, especially on these early morning calls, wear some thicker soled shoes so your feet won't freeze.

Bring a big coat to keep warm between shots.

Of course, on these hot days try to stay cool, stay out of the sun and drink lots of water.

7. **Parents, if you're driving, fill up the tank** the day before and get parking instructions. If using public transportation have your **fare ready and your route planned.**

8. **Be on time.** Figure out your travel time based on distance and traffic at that hour, and plan to arrive at least 15 minutes prior to your call. Being late is bad news.

9. **Check in with the AD.** When you arrive on the set, find the AD (Assistant Director) and let him/her know you're there. He or she will lead you to the teacher / social worker, make-up, wardrobe.

10. **Be cooperative.** Everyone you're working with has been hired to put their talents together to shoot the commercial. Working in a positive, cooperative way helps to make doing the job much easier.

Listen and follow directions and always try to do what you're asked to do right away. Take directions only from the director and if you have a problem, ask questions. If you mess up, work it out so you can do it right the next time.

Watch your behavior on the set and try to stay quiet and still. Minimize the playing, after all, it's a job and you're there to do what? Work. This doesn't mean it can't be fun because you should enjoy your work. Also be aware that sets can be very dangerous, so be careful and stay clear of wires and hot lights, etc.

Conserve your energy. The day or days can be very long and tedious so to keep from 'pooping out' later in the day and maybe becoming irritable, just stay cool and calm and take it slow, so you can save some energy for the rest of the day.

TECHNICALLY SPEAKING

Commercials are very technical. Most of the direction you get will have to do with technical things like:
　　–Hitting your marks
　　–Finding your light
　　–Cheating to camera
　　–Timing

Even if you do a wonderful performance on a *take*, if it's not technically correct then it's no good. You may be technically incorrect or it may be another technical problem. In any case a lot of time and takes can be wasted so it's important to be aware of what you are doing. Now let's review these techniques.

• **HITTING YOUR MARK**

Marks are specific spots where you are to
Stop
Stand
Move to
Place a product on

Remember, in doing the slate, we had a mark on the floor on which you were to stand.
During the actual shooting of the commercial, marks are crucial, otherwise you could be
　　–blocking someone or something
　　–causing the product to be out of focus
　　–just in the wrong place

So pay close attention to your marks and practice hitting them so that you can do it correctly and work it into your other moves and/or dialogue.

• **FINDING YOUR LIGHT**

When you have been placed on a mark there is a light or lights that shine on your face. Try to feel this light on your face and don't move in and out of it casting a shadow on your face.
If you're handling the product, you also have to be aware of the

light that is shining on it.

Hitting and staying on your marks will help you to find and stay in your light.

• CHEATING TO CAMERA

We talked about this technique in Part II during auditions, but it is especially important during filming. When you are to relate to others in the scene, be aware of directing your activity and dialogue in favor of the camera's eye so that your action is seen by the camera and you do not upstage yourself.

Example: If you're talking to someone to the side of you, instead of looking directly at them, let your eyes go to them, but keep your face and body angled toward the camera. Sometimes the director will even suggest that you don't really even look at the person, but 'cheat the look' and just look in their general direction. The cheat is not noticed by the camera's eye.

Illustration:

Instead of this: Do this:

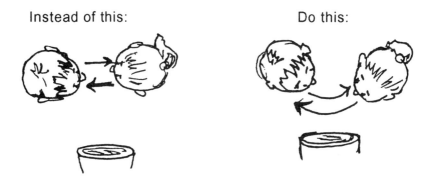

You may also be asked to cheat the product to camera. The same principle applies. Angle the product towards the camera's eye. Any marks you've been given should go along with this move.

• TIMING

Most commercials are :30 or :60 seconds. Not much time to get your whole point across. Usually you have less time than that to do what you are directed to do so you need to focus – speak clearly – and keep it moving.

All of your actions are affected by time. They should be specific and done "on time.'

If you have a lot of dialogue, use your diaphragm. Let the air drop in quickly without gasping and control the amount coming out with the stomach muscles, so you can say lots of dialogue on one breath. Make sure you articulate and try not to sound rushed.

Picking up your cues when you have dialogue with someone else is a major part of doing the commercial 'on time.'

Be careful of overlapping though, which means coming in too quickly before the other person finishes speaking. Each line has to be clean and clear for editing.

• BEATS

These are mentally counted seconds before a cue. A director will often tell you to "wait two beats before entering", "count three beats before you say your line", etc. This means that you basically count 2 or 3 seconds in your head before your cue or action.

• 'CUT'

Continue your action in the commercial and stay in character until the director says 'cut'. Don't assume that once you've stopped speaking, the filming is over. Hold! Until you hear 'Cut.' You can ruin a take by breaking too soon.

• EATING

If you are doing a commercial in which you are supposed to be eating something, first of all, make sure it is something that you will and can eat before you accept the job. If it's something that you really don't like or physically are not supposed to have, then just pass on it. Don't even go on the audition because if you get the job, you may have to eat a lot of it on the set.

But even if you like it, don't 'pig–out'. You may have to do a lot of takes and you don't want to get too full or even sick.

During the shooting when you take a bite of the product, after they say 'cut' you can spit it out in a bag or bucket that they give you. I know this doesn't sound too appetizing but 'enough is enough' , so don't be ashamed to get rid of it or think it's so delicious that you'll never get enough because you will.

YOUR PERFORMANCE

• REPETITION

For the director to get the right 'feel' he wants for the spot, all the moves correct, and the timing exact, you may have to repeat your performance, what may seem like a hundred times.

Don't be surprised, get irritable, or robot-like.

Often times you won't know why you have to do it again. Just try to give the same performance with the same energy and freshness as the first one, unless of course, you're directed otherwise.

If your performance becomes robotic, then it will be difficult to add colors or make adjustments.

So when asked to do it again, forget that you've done it 50 times already. Just go for it like it's your first time through <u>being fresh and natural</u> but <u>technically</u> remembering all the directions.

• BE CREATIVE

The more relaxed and focused you are, the more creative you can be. Often times, once they get what they want, they will ask you to do something different. Trust yourself, open up, and don't be afraid to try different things. You'll be surprised what kind of genius can come out of you, if you have confidence, and are relaxed enough to let the creative juices flow. This doesn't mean take it all the way out and start doing strange or silly things, but it does mean coloring your performance with different attitudes and inflections, while staying focused, being believable and real. Even though you're being creative and trying different things, make sure you still do your performance within the time frame of the spot.

• MAKING MISTAKES

If you mess up during a take, don't get upset or silly or start apologizing over and over. **EXCUSE YOURSELF, CALM DOWN, THEN CORRECT YOURSELF.** Even if you joke about it, remember that you still have to correct it, and put it straight in your mind before you go on. Be aware that it is more difficult to say a line or do an action correctly when you've flubbed it on the previous take.

Take a few minutes to practice it right. If it is a problem with dialogue, repeat it several times and straighten it out before you say you're ready to go on. It's okay, people make mistakes all the time, so don't be hard on yourself, and at the same time, work on it so it won't take forever to correct it.

- **GOOD GRIEF, WHEN WILL WE GET THROUGH?**

When the day drags on and on, and it seems like they don't know what they're doing and you wonder if you'll ever go home again, just remember that you actually won't be there forever, and after the shoot is over, your job is finished and you can soon collect residuals that you can save for all the things you want to do in life. That should help ease the pain.

- **STAY READY**

After you've done your first commercial, you should be proud of yourself, but don't stop working on yourself. Keep practicing. Stay toned up and ready. There's plenty of competition out there and lots of kids go up for the same jobs, so make sure your tools stay sharp. You've got to keep your body, speech, and performance ability in tone and ready for the next audition and the next job.

- **STAY IN TOUCH WITH YOUR AGENCY**

Visit them now and then so they can see you and be reminded of your wonderful self and any changes in you. Also, you get to see their faces, establish closer relationships, and meet any new people working there. Be friends with your agents, and stay in touch with them, keeping them abreast of all address and phone number changes, too.

The more auditions and commercials you do, the more experience you will have and knowledge you will gain. Keep these two points in mind:
  * Accept, correct, and learn from your mistakes.
  * Recognize, enjoy, and grow from your experiences.

Chapter 4

...And Much More!

- Print
- Voice Overs
- Survival Tips

PRINT – MODELING

A print ad is the commercial advertising you see in magazines, newspapers, on posters and billboards. For this, they use commercial actors or models. Models also do catalog work for various clothing stores and photo shoots for all sorts of designer and fashion ads.

To do print work you need to be:

expressive
animated
and love taking pictures

If you desire to do print work, find out if your agency has a print department. If so, when you meet with them, they will be able to see if you have what it takes. They will also let you know what you need as far as pictures. Usually,

1.   a composite – or zed card with several different looks. (see example)

2.   portfolio/book – containing professional full size pictures of you and any ads that you have done.

For Print Jobs that you do, the agents will give you Time Sheets to be filled out and turned into them when you work, so they can keep track of your jobs, hours and make sure you get paid. The same holds true for modeling jobs.

SUNDE JOHNSON

HEIGHT: 57" / SIZE: 10-12 / HAIR: Brown / EYES: Brown / BIRTHDATE: 03-30-83

PHOTOS BY NANCY JO GILCHRIST

L.A. Talent

L.A. TALENT PRINT, 8335 SUNSET, LOS ANGELES, CA 90069, (213) 656-3981, FAX: (213) 656-0489

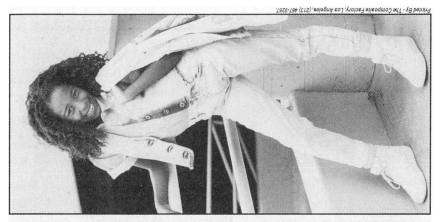

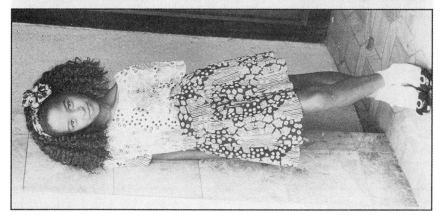

JESSE BARLET

HAIR   **RED**

EYES   **HAZEL**

D.O.B.   **3-31-82**

S.S. #

L.A. MODELS/L.A. TALENT

L.A. MODELS • 8335 SUNSET BLVD., LOS ANGELES, CA 90069

KIDS DIVISION (213) 656-9572 • FAX (213) 656-0489 / L.A. TALENT (213) 656-3722 • FAX (213) 650-4272

There is a difference between Print and Modeling.
To model, you should be:
>> well proportioned
>> have a slender, toned figure
>> have a pretty or handsome face

Models do:
>> —print
>> —fashion
>> —catalog
>> —runway

and are represented by a Model Agency, who take 20% or more of their earnings as commission.

For print work, you can be:
>> —more real, 'kid next door' looking
>> —cute with lots of personality
>> —a character type

Print departments can be found at modeling agencies and some commercial agencies. They also take 20% or more of your earnings as commission. There are no unions for print or modeling, so pay amounts and commissions vary according to the model's experience and the usage of the ad. There are no residuals in print and no tax taken out until the end of the year.

An interview for a Print Job is sometimes called a 'Go See'.
On the 'Go See' always bring along a picture or composite and portfolio or book if you have one. They may talk to you a little and look at your book or they may just take a polaroid. So here the polaroid is very important. It should be:

>> very expressive
>> animated
>> with lots of energy behind the eyes

A photograph freezes time and what we see is what you are thinking and feeling at the moment. So even though it's a picture, you need to be specific about your thoughts and what you visually project to the camera. There are times when you'll get some direction as to what you are to be thinking and/or feeling in the shot. So LISTEN carefully, and try to FOCUS and EXPRESS your thoughts with your eyes, face, and body language.

This does not mean making faces but having real, believable thoughts relating to the direction you're given.

On a big print campaign you may be put on video where you are asked to improvise a situation relating to what the job will be. These print interviews are sometimes just called auditions.

If you're not given a specific direction for the polaroid, all you can do is relax, think a good thought, and give a nice smile with expressive eyes.

If you know that it is going to be a very animated ad, make the smile and eyes a little brighter, but not too much. You don't want to look strange.

If you have to use props try to make your holding positions seem natural.

• THE SHOOT

Even though it is still photography, the job is not at all easy. You may take a couple of hundred pictures or more during the session and each one should have life.

It is easy for your face to become stiff and your motions stilted.
To Stay Fresh:
— Shake out and do some stretches between shots.
— Use your facial exercises to loosen up your face.
— Blow out between your lips on BRRR.
— Do some natural moves between shots then relax into your holding positions.

There is a lot of repetition in print work and if you start to feel like you're pushing it, ask the photographer for a short break.

When you finish don't forget to:
— Fill out your time sheet and have it signed.
— Collect all of your belongings.
— Find out when and where the ad will be shown, so that you can get a copy for your portfolio.

So for print work you have to **have energy, be animated, and like taking pictures.**

VOICE OVERS (VO)

Voice Overs include the voices you hear on radio spots, over TV commercials, and cartoon characters. It is a very tight field and a lot of kids voices are done by adults. However, there are kids who do voice over work and usually they

- can speak clearly and read copy quickly
- interpret copy very well
- have expressive voices
- are able to add different attitudes and color to their tones.
- have animated voices with a special quality like a high pitch, squeaky voice or husky voice, etc.
- can maintain and recreate a voice quality as needed
- know how to use their diaphragm (Pg. 7)

If you have these qualities and want to do voice overs, see if your agency has a voice over department. They may ask you to get a demo tape done.

• **DEMO TAPE**

This is a professionally done tape, with a variety of your voices, that represents your abilities as a VO artist.

- Demo tapes are sent out to casting directors who, in turn, may call for you to audition or may just cast you from the tape.
- The people who put these together for you are found in the trades papers or your agent can refer you.
  Before making the investment, check out their work, listen to some demos they've done and compare prices.
  They should have lots of different copy and background music to help you put together a professional tape. Here is some work you can do at home to prepare and give you some ideas.

To prepare yourself for a demo tape:
Record yourself at home reading from
- ads in magazines, newspapers
- commercials

- books
- scripts
- something you create

Recall the voice work we did in Chapter 1:
- working from the diaphragm
- using all the levels of your voice

Create different voices
- the young announcer
  from straight forward to energetic
- character types you play or would like to play including more animated cartoon voices. You can come up with different sounds by holding your tongue and lips in certain positions and/or by making dramatic changes in your voice pitch.
- read with different attitudes or emotions. Use background music. It should help you add color and levels to your voice.

Then listen to yourself.

1. Correcting any nicks in your voice, paying special attention to enunciation, inflections, and breath control. Since the microphone will be very close to you while recording, you should not hear yourself take a breath between phrases. So you have to really use that diaphragm and let the air drop in, instead of gasping.

2. Be especially aware of two consonants, 's' and 'p'. Microphones are very sensitive to them, so don't hiss the 's's or pop the 'p's.

3. Test your ability to maintain each voice and recreate it at a later time. Record different voices then go back later and try to repeat them. If you can't remember what you were doing, use your tape to review.

The above exercises help you to:
- Make your voice flexible.
- Become familiar with your different voice tones.
- Realize what it takes to maintain and recall different voices.

• 'J' CARDS, MAILINGS

It is up to you how much you're willing to invest based on your desire, your pocketbook, and you potential as a VO artist.

In addition to the actual cost of the demo tape production, there are additional costs for: reproductions of the tape, printing of 'J' cards (which go inside the cassette jacket with your name, voice qualifications, agent info, and your picture on it, if you wish) you can also do mailings to advertising agencies and casting directors, sending them your demo tape.

• WORKSHOPS

There are reputable voice over workshops that you can join to develop your voice talents. They can also help to network you into the business. The majority of VO workshops are taught by producers and casting directors in the VO industry. If you're good, the word can get out and you can begin to work quickly. It all depends on your talent.

Of course you don't have to join a workshop. You can do as I have done, work on yourself liked we discussed in the section.

SURVIVAL TIPS

- **PARENTS — YOUR PART**

As in everything involving your children, most of the work and responsibility falls on you. Not only do you have to prepare your child, but you must be aware of and prepare yourself for the extra work, time, and commitment involved. The law of averages applies to kids too. If you can't find a sitter, you, your child, and your other children if any, may have to go on a lot of calls before the child books a spot. We all hope our child will "hit" right away, but you must be prepared to "pay some dues". This means:

1. Creativity

2. Patience

3. Endurance

4. Planning Ahead (and then some)

1. Creativity:

You have to use your creative imagination and energy in working with your child. Make the work interesting and exciting, but at the same time help the child to develop good technique and a professional attitude.

2. Patience:

A very important element. Not only the patience as a parent, but as a teacher, and friend. Understand that the creative process works best in a relaxed, positive atmosphere. While helping your child develop the discipline it takes to be a good actor and to accomplish their goals, don't ever force the issue. Work only as long as you can work positively and the child remains interested and energetic. Keep creating new approaches toward the work. Be aware not to put pressure on the child or to make acting time a task. Keep it fun, and once the child becomes involved in an acting class, stay in touch and involved with the activities of the class. If during an audition or a job, the child makes a mistake, don't chastise them, but teach them how to correct, work out, and learn from their mistakes.

3. Endurance:

Aside from the grind of the auditioning process, when the child books a job, the rewards are great, but you and your child will be on set for a good part of the day. You'll have to schedule your life around that and be prepared for it. Unless your child prefers and can handle a lot of independence, be available for your child at all times. There will be a social worker on set to watch over your children but you should always be responsible for your child. You or a guardian must be on set the entire time the child is there.

Stay out of the way of the work situation, but stay close enough to watch what's going on. Don't get so involved in socializing or supposedly 'making contacts' that you are unconscious of your child's needs and whereabouts. Also, remember that parts of the set can be *very dangerous.* There is a lot of electrical equipment, unstable objects, and also valuable props. We know how curious children can be, so we must keep that "special eye" open.

4. Planning Ahead:

For auditioning, this means finding sitters, preparing proper dinners, and caring for your whole family in less amounts of time, because you must take time out to go to auditions. Make sure you have the right directions and address to the audition and be prepared for a long crowded wait. This is not always the case and be thankful if it's not. Whether summer or winter, realize how cool it turns in the evenings, since you may still be out, and bring a sweater or jacket for the child and yourself, although we know you'll survive. Have small quiet toys for your baby, along with extra bottles and changes of clothes. Like I said in Chapter 2, older kids should take their homework along in case they have time to get some of it done. If school is out, take a book or non-messy, quiet game or activity. Carry along a snack (low or no sugar) and of course, their tools – picture, resumé and social security number. Also, remember to keep the work permit up to date in case your child books a job.

Traveling by car is easier because you can throw the whole house in there (which my husband says I do anyway) but the kids and I always have enough stuff. It's a lot of work but it's worth it because when they're happy, I'm happy.

Make sure you unload when you get home or else your car will become unbearable. Even if you've packed a couple of bags and used public transportation, unpack when you get home. Putting things back to normal helps finish the experience and enables you to get on with your life.

- **SUGGESTED SNACKS**

Fruit	Crackers	Carrots –or–
Fruit Juice	Low Salt Chips	Celery sticks

Not having to make extra stops for treats or snacks saves time, hassle and money.

On-set, food is provided and the social worker has school material and often some games. However, it's still good to bring your child's favorite snack, toy, and/or activity. This way they can do something familiar or have a special treat.

- **TEACH YOUR KIDS GOOD HABITS**

If all you give them are healthy snacks, you'll be surprised. They start asking for them. Giving them a lot of sugar and processed foods changes their temperament. I've seen parents give their children a piece of candy or a cookie and then tell them to go sit down somewhere. They may sit for a while, while they're eating it, but then the sugar starts working and they're flying. The parent starts fussing, then the child gets irritable because their blood is rushing and the whole situation is unhealthy and unnecessary. As I suggested before, try some fresh fruit and fresh vegetables or some low salt popcorn and plenty of water. If they complain about water, give them half juice and half water all the time. At least they're getting some water. Sometimes they'll even ask for water, but never give them soda instead.

The emotional changes a child goes through in this business are enough without having to compound them with a unhealthy diet.

Teach them how to control their emotions and their reactions to situations. Setting a good example is the best teacher. Rejection should not be seen as a personal putdown. There are many reasons they may not get a job, most of them having nothing to do with their performance. One of the main reasons is, they may not look like what is needed, or match with someone else.

For a child to get a job, it is a great accomplishment, but remember the work doesn't stop there. *If a child becomes too busy or too self-indulgent in the business, slow their participation down or put a halt to it until things are put back into proper perspective.* Involvement in this business is only okay if you and your child are happy and the results are productive.

There is also a wonderful handbook with a lot more valuable information for young people that AFTRA and SAG have put out together and is available at your union office. It's called "The AFTRA/SAG Young Performers Handbook."

THE FINALE

We've covered quite a bit in this book. You've learned how to prepare and keep yourselves in a "ready to go get 'em" state. You've learned about your diaphragm, and how to use it to control your energy and voice. You've learned how to break down copy, how to act on auditions, and how to act on set. You've also learned new words, all of which you can find in the Glossary. This, like many other workbooks, should be carried around with you as part of you "stuff," until you become really familiar with it's contents, and your techniques become second nature. Like anything worth having, a successful commercial career takes time to develop. So stay in a positive frame of mind, accepting and learning from your experiences and always looking forward to reaching higher levels professionally and spiritually. Pray a lot, recognize and be thankful for your many blessings and stay focused. Now get to work. I love you. God bless you, and see you on the set !

Glossary

action
> 1. Your Movement within the scene.
> 2. Your cue to perform.

action cue
> The point at which you begin to perform – on the word "action".

AD
> An abbreviation for assistant director. The person you check in with when you arrive on set, and the person who should know your whereabouts at all times on set.

ad
> An abbreviation of advertisement. A photographed advertisement for a product or service.

ad lib
> Speech or action that has not been written or specifically rehearsed.

AFTRA
> American Federation of Television and Radio Artists. A talent union that covers video tape productions, voice overs and radio.

agent
> A person or group of persons that represent talent and are paid a commission. They are responsible for submitting you on jobs and negotiating your contracts. They should be franchised by SAG.

audition
> Also known as an "interview" or "call" in which an actor/actress performs before a client in hopes of getting a job. The actor/actress may be required to read lines from a script, do pantomime, improvisation, and in general perform for the purpose of showing his/her qualifications for a role.

beats
Moments or seconds counted mentally before a cue, or before continuing action.

Book – Booked
A job confirmation, meaning you get the job.

Callback
A request for a talent to return for an additional audition for the same client and the same job. Those competing for the job have been reduced in number. The actor is paid for the 2nd callback (3rd call in all) and any more thereafter.

Call time
A specified time at which the talent should arrive on set. The call time is usually earlier than the "on set call time" to allow for make-up and wardrobing.

Call sheet
A form specifying what is to be shot and all the personnel and equipment required to film on a certain day.

camera left
The left side from the camera's eye. If you were facing the camera, it would be your right.

camera right
The right side from the camera's eye. If you were facing the camera, it would be your left. [Camera left and right are the opposite of stage left and right.]

case history
The life history you create for your character that coincides

with the facts in the play and your relationship to the other characters.

casting director – CD
The person in charge of the casting session, representing the producer, and is responsible for choosing talent to audition for the producer and client.

center
Your center of energy. The area around and including the diaphragm.

character
A reference to the person you represent in the acting situation.

characterization
To give background, life, expression, behavior, colors, and motivation to the person you are portraying in an acting situation.

cheat the look
This term is used so that the camera can get a better picture. Instead of looking directly at someone or something, (which causes you to turn away from camera) you instead look in that general direction but favor the camera's eye more.

cheat to camera
The same explanation as above but not just in reference to a look, but anything in the camera's eye favoring the camera.

client
The person/people who represent the advertising company for which the commercial is being done.

close-up/CU
A very tight shot of a performer or an object, showing more detail.

cold reading
An unrehearsed reading of a script, usually at auditions.

composite
A set of pictures of a talent on one sheet, maybe two sides, with a headshot and several other different looks. It may also contain some talent statistics and the agent's logo.

contact sheet
A photo sheet of usually one roll of film from which you choose the pictures to be enlarged.

copy
The script of a commercial or voice over.

copy breakdown
The analyzing of a script for the purpose of getting it to performance level.

creative dialogue
Speaking, relating a story or event, fact or fiction, and continuing non-stop for any given amount of time.

CU
Close-up.

cue
A verbal or visible signal for you to begin to speak and/or act.

cue cards
Large white cards (approx. 2' x 2-1/2') with the copy printed on it large enough to be read at a distance during an audition.

cut
A verbal or visible cue for the performer to stop speaking and/or acting, given by the director.

cycle
A thirteen week period of time in which a commercial is used or put on hold.

date book
> A well-organized, dated book or electronic organizer containing your appointments, auditions, phone numbers, addresses and pertinent information you need for the business.

demo tapes
> A variety of commercials or voice over work done in a professional manner that represents your abilities as a artist.

diaphragm
> A body partition of muscle separating the chest and abdominal cavity that expands and releases as air goes in and out of the lungs.

directions
> Instruction and guidance on the action or conduct of a performer given by a director.

external
> A surface performance with no real feeling behind it.

fitting
> A scheduled time and place for the talent to be wardrobed for a commercial.

first position
> In ballet, a position in which the heels are together, feet

turned out, legs are turned out from the hip while squeezing the inside of the thighs together.

first refusal
A client would like to reserve the right to hire or refuse you for a job on a certain day if you are offered another job.

flippers
False teeth for children that are used for cosmetic purposes and easily removed.

focus
To give your full, undivided attention to what you are doing.

frame
The area of vision that is actually seen on TV. This is usually smaller than the camera's vision and marked off in the viewer. (Although, not on your everyday camera)

gaffer
A lighting director or the person who places lighting instruments.

hitting your mark
Stopping your action at a specific point that has been determined by the director.

improv
An abbreviation for improvisation. An unrehearsed performance done on the spur of the moment. (You may be given the overall situation and some direction, but the action and dialogue are unscripted and unrehearsed.)

"J card"
A title card that fits into a cassette tape holder with your information and agency on it.

law of averages
A working theory that out of so many attempts to get a job, you will actually book a certain percentage.

mailings
Packages containing your picture, resumé, and cover letter or announcements of an upcoming performance that is mailed to agents and/or casting directors for either representation or showcasing of talent.

manager
A person who supervises and is responsible for the career of

the talent they represent. They work on a commission basis and on a more personal level than an agent.

mark
1. An exact place on the floor that the actor must stand on or stop at as directed. It is usually indicated by tape.
2. An exact place where a product or object is to be put, or where an action is to take place.

mic
An abbreviation for microphone.

mime
The art of acting out a situation or action without words or props.

monologue
A solo performance by an actor.

MOS
Mit out sound. There is no sound being recorded during filming. (It's from the Germans and it's mit because they couldn't pronounce "with").

motivation
Your reason for saying or doing what you're doing.

MOW
A television movie of the week.

on avail
The client is checking your availability for a certain day, but has made no final decisions.

one liners
An acting assignment that involves a single line or phrase.

on location
A designated place other than a sound stage to film a commercial.

out clause
A clause written into the contract that allows you to get out of the contract if certain terms aren't met.

out of frame
Performance or action that cannot be seen within the television frame.

PA
An abbreviation for production assistant, a person on set who is available to assist you, as talent or the production crew in any way possible.

pantomime
Conveying an object or an action without the use of props.

"P & G Look"
P & G stands for Proctor & Gamble. The look is very 'middle of the road', neat, well groomed, and casual.

pick up cues
To come in on time with your action or speech.

print
A photographed advertisement of a person, product, and/or service.

producer
The creator and/or organizer of the commercial. (Usually in charge of financial matters).

product
The object or service being advertised.

production company
　　The company responsible for the actual making of the commercial.

professional
　　One who knows his/her craft and is paid a comparable salary for it.

profile
　　A side view of your face and/or body.

program use
　　The use of a commercial during an actual program.　The product is the sponsor of such program.　Talent is paid for each program use.

proofsheet
　　See 'CONTACT SHEET'.

props
　　Objects which are set or carried in a scene.

repertoire
　　A list of dramatic pieces which you can perform.

reproductions
　　Professionally made copies of your picture(s) with your name and maybe the agents logo on them.

residuals
　　Payments to the talent for the usage of a commercial in which he/she has been a principal performer.

resumé
　　A professional, typed, list of your credits, training, union affiliation, and skills.

"Roll Tape" / "Roll 'em'"
A verbal cue to start recording on tape or exposing film.

SAG
Screen Actors Guild. Talent union which covers all jobs done on film.

second position
In ballet, a position where the feet are approximately shoulder length apart and turned out. Second position for the arms is up and out to the sides, slightly rounded at the elbow, (like you're holding a huge ball) with the shoulders pressed down.

sense memory
Being able to recall and demonstrate the particulars of an object, situation, or condition in it's absence.

set
1. A designated area where the commercial is being shot.
2. The area of performance including furnishings and props.

shooting
The actual filming of the commercial.

shot has to match
This means that the piece that is presently being filmed has to match a previous shot as far as hair, make-up, position of talent, and props on the set.

sign-in sheet
A form distributed by SAG or AFTRA and provided by the casting director on which the talent signs in on arrival, giving the required information and signs out on departure.

size card / size sheet
A card or sheet provided by the casting director and filled out by talent on request, giving name, address, phone numbers,

measurements, ss#, etc. A polaroid of talent is often stapled to this sheet or card.

slate
The opening shot taped in an audition where the talent states their name, and if requested, their age and agency.

spot
The commercial being auditioned for, or being filmed.

stepping on lines
Saying your lines before another actor has completed his. Therefore, not leaving space for clear editing.

storyboard
A printed sheet including pictures of the planned shot setups, and the corresponding dialogue for a particular commercial.

take / takes
A completed recorded version of the action and/or dialogue being filmed or taped.

talent
The performer, actor, or actress.

theatrical agent
An agency that represents talent for feature films, television shows, stage plays, movies of the week, etc.

3/4 Shot
Picture showing not just the head but a portion of the body.

tools
The skills and equipment you need to work as a professional in the commercial business.

trades
Publications that deal with the entertainment industry, i.e. Variety, Backstage, Drama-Logue, Hollywood Reporter, etc.

transition
   A change in thought, mood, or attitude.

union
   An organization that represents talent and protects their rights i.e., SAG, AFTRA, AEA (Actors Equity Association - Theatre)

unit
   Each city is given a certain number of units according to it's population. These units are figured in determining your pay for the usage of the commercial.

upstage
   1. The area of the stage closer to the back curtain or back drop.
   2. Overshadowing someone else's performance by mugging, stepping on lines, blocking them, or messing up direction. (Not a nice thing to do)

voice over
   Off camera dialogue, radio spots, voices of cartoon characters.

wardrobe call
   A designated time and place for the talent to be fitted in the wardrobe to be worn in the commercial.

weather permits
If the weather is favorable the commercial will be shot.

wildspot use
Usage of a commercial broadcast by non-interconnected single situations, a use that is independent of any program or is used on local participating programs.

"Wind it up" / "Wrap it up"
A visual or verbal cue to bring dialogue and action to a finish.

work permit (entertainment)
A legal document issued by the state granting a minor permission to work.

wrap
Refers to the completion of work on a particular set, sequence, or location.

xylophone
A musical instrument. Has nothing to do with this book.

X
Your mark. Where you should stand, stop, look, place an object, etc.

Yes
The preferred answer to the question, "Did I book the job?"

"Zed card"
  A smaller composite geared more toward fashion, or a folded
  8-1/2" x 11" sheet with various looks.